# The Beauty of Salvation

Copyright © 2021 by Add to Your Faith Publications

All rights reserved. No part of this book may be reproduced or transmitted in any form or by any means without permission in writing from the author.

Published in Wakefield, RI, by Add to Your Faith Publications.

All Scripture is taken from the King James Bible.

ISBN: 978-1-7370357-2-5

Printed and Bound in the United States of America.

# The Beauty of Salvation

## MARVEL AT GOD'S UNSPEAKABLE GIFT

Paul E. Chapman

# Table of Contents

Introduction ...................................................................... 7
1. The Beauty of Salvation ............................................... 11
2. The Beauty of Conception ........................................... 19
3. The Beauty of Adoption ............................................... 27
4. The Beauty of Redemption .......................................... 35
5. The Beauty of Regeneration ........................................ 45
6. The Beauty of Reconciliation ....................................... 55
7. The Beauty of Remission ............................................. 63
8. The Beauty of Imputation ............................................ 75
9. The Beauty of Propitiation ........................................... 85
10. The Beauty of Justification .......................................... 89
11. The Beauty of Sanctification ........................................ 99
12. The Beauty of Glorification ........................................ 109
Afterword: 5 Steps to Heaven ........................................ 123

# Introduction

Salvation is beautiful. Although we can opine about the theological perfection of the doctrines of salvation, we must never forget the beauty of it.

I was born again at a youth revival on a Saturday evening. It was the second night of a two-day youth revival at the Blessed Hope Baptist Church in Jasonville, Indiana. I remember it as if it were yesterday. Friday night, the guest preacher (who would eventually become my youth pastor) preached a message entitled "Watching Jesus Die." It seemed as though I were sitting on a hillside watching Christ go through every moment of the Crucifixion.

On the next night, he preached on Hell. I could smell the sulfur and hear the crackling of the flames. I put my faith in Christ that evening. Praise God, I have never been the same! I went to bed that night with the perfect peace of knowing that if I did not wake up in this life, I would be in Heaven with God. I was saved from Hell! I was born again as a child of God! What an unspeakable gift!

My salvation is just as real and as precious as it was that first night. Hallelujah, my eternal life has barely begun! Why then do I take my salvation for granted at times? You know what I mean. It is human nature. Familiarity can breed contempt or, at the least, disregard. If you have been saved for a while, you probably have been there. The joy of salvation fades. Service that was once a privilege becomes drudgery. In the past, your eyes would fill with tears quickly at God's goodness, but how long has it been since you wept over God's love and care for you? It probably has been too long.

# THE BEAUTY OF SALVATION

Years ago, I heard an old preacher say, "Some of you have been saved too long." I understood his meaning immediately. He was saying that some believers were too far removed from their salvation. They had forgotten what it was like to be lost. The miracle of salvation had not waned in its effectiveness, but its impact in their consciousnesses had faded.

Often, I remind our congregation, "Don't get too far away from the Cross. Visit Calvary often. Relive your salvation. Remember that you should be in Hell. Recall the miracle of forgiveness and eternal life so freely given by the amazing grace of God." Our Lord knows that we are a forgetful people. He warned us to remember on purpose, lest we forget, what is most important.

**Deuteronomy 4:9**
*Only take heed to thyself, and keep thy soul diligently, lest thou forget the things which thine eyes have seen, and lest they depart from thy heart all the days of thy life: but teach them thy sons, and thy sons' sons;*

**Deuteronomy 6:12**
*Then beware lest thou forget the LORD, which brought thee forth out of the land of Egypt, from the house of bondage.*

**Deuteronomy 8:11–14**
*Beware that thou forget not the LORD thy God, in not keeping his commandments, and his judgments, and his statutes, which I command thee this day: Lest when thou hast eaten and art full, and hast built goodly houses, and dwelt therein; And when thy herds and thy flocks multiply, and thy silver and thy gold is multiplied, and all that thou hast is multiplied; Then thine heart be lifted up, and thou forget the LORD thy God, which brought thee forth out of the land of Egypt, from the house of bondage;*

**Psalm 103:2**
*Bless the LORD, O my soul, and forget not all his benefits:*

**Proverbs 3:1**
*My son, forget not my law; but let thine heart keep my commandments:*

# INTRODUCTION

**Proverbs 4:5**
*Get wisdom, get understanding: forget it not; neither decline from the words of my mouth.*

**Hosea 4:6**
*My people are destroyed for lack of knowledge: because thou hast rejected knowledge, I will also reject thee, that thou shalt be no priest to me: seeing thou hast forgotten the law of thy God, I will also forget thy children.*

**Matthew 16:9**
*Do ye not yet understand, neither remember the five loaves of the five thousand, and how many baskets ye took up?*

**Mark 8:18**
*Having eyes, see ye not? and having ears, hear ye not? and do ye not remember?*

These verses are only a sampling of what the Scriptures teach about our need to remember and not forget. It would be very instructive for each of us to perform a word study using those words in Scripture. How quickly we forget! Jehovah lamented the waning of love of the Israelites.

**Jeremiah 2:2-5**
*Go and cry in the ears of Jerusalem, saying, Thus saith the LORD; I remember thee, the kindness of thy youth, the love of thine espousals, when thou wentest after me in the wilderness, in a land that was not sown. Israel was holiness unto the LORD, and the firstfruits of his increase: all that devour him shall offend; evil shall come upon them, saith the LORD. Hear ye the word of the LORD, O house of Jacob, and all the families of the house of Israel: Thus saith the LORD, What iniquity have your fathers found in me, that they are gone far from me, and have walked after vanity, and are become vain?*

# THE BEAUTY OF SALVATION

How sad! Can you sense the pain of the Lord in these verses? He compares His relationship with Israel to that of a married couple. I have seen the scenario many times throughout the years. A couple is so excited to get married. They cannot get enough of each other. They stand at an altar and pledge their undying love. They plan to live happily ever after. Over time, the newness of marriage wanes. They realize how busy life really is. They barely talk unless it is about business or to argue. They are like roommates rather than love birds. What happened to the exciting love of their engagement and early years of marriage? Do not let that sad story happen to your relationship with God!

While regeneration is theologically perfect and impressive in its technicalities, we must never lose the awe of God's love for us. Although, there are duties in the Christian life, we must never become so bogged down by our activities that we neglect the incredible privilege of having an intimate relationship with God.

This book is written to remind us that salvation is beautiful. I pray that as you read it, there will be many times when your eyes moisten with tears. I hope that you will put the book down occasionally and marvel at God's love for you. Our salvation is beautiful!

## Chapter One

# The Beauty of Salvation

As we begin our journey of remembering our salvation, let us consider four reasons that salvation is beautiful.

### 1. The Beauty of Salvation's Story

Everyone enjoys a good love story. You know the plot. Someone loves someone else, but there is a reason the lovebirds cannot be together. Finally, they overcome the obstacle; and the lovers live happily ever after. Can you hear the sniffles of someone crying?

Famous books recount great love stories. Megahit movies have raked in millions by helping star-crossed lovers find one another. The Hallmark Channel makes endless movies with the same plot. They just change the names and the seasons! However, there is one tale of love that makes them all pale in comparison. The Gospel is the greatest love story ever told.

**John 3:16**
*For God so loved the world, that he gave his only begotten Son, that whosoever believeth in him should not perish, but have everlasting life.*

God loves you! But you cannot be together with God because of sin. Our Lord made a way of salvation by sacrificing Himself so that we could be together with Him. The salvation love story is told in many different ways in Scripture, but the plot is the same. God loves humanity and wants to spend eternity with them, but they are separated from Him because of sin. In fact, mankind is dying. God loves them so much that He sacrificed His most prized possession to rescue them. Through salvation, God and man can live happily ever after!

The unfathomable love of God is foreshadowed in many stories of love in Scripture. Consider a few of them here.

In Song of Solomon, we are told a story with colorful, veiled language of two people who truly loved one another. The word *love* is used twenty-five times in the eight short chapters of Solomon's song. Consider the emotion in these verses from the book.

**Song of Solomon 6:4**
*Thou art beautiful, O my love, as Tirzah, comely as Jerusalem, terrible as an army with banners.*

**Song of Solomon 8:6–7**
*Set me as a seal upon thine heart, as a seal upon thine arm: for love is strong as death; jealousy is cruel as the grave: the coals thereof are coals of fire, which hath a most vehement flame. Many waters cannot quench love, neither can the floods drown it: if a man would give all the substance of his house for love, it would utterly be contemned.*

In Genesis 29, we learn of Jacob, who worked fourteen years for his true love, Rachel. His love and commitment to her is a picture of God's love.

**Genesis 29:20–28**
*And Jacob served seven years for Rachel; and they seemed unto him but a few days, for the love he had to her. And Jacob said unto Laban, Give me my wife, for my days are fulfilled, that I may go in unto her. And Laban gathered together all the men of the place, and made a feast. And it came to pass in the evening, that he took Leah his daughter, and brought her to him; and he went in unto her. And Laban gave unto his daughter Leah Zilpah his maid for an handmaid. And it came to pass, that in the morning, behold, it was Leah: and he said to Laban, What is this thou hast done unto me? did not I serve with thee for Rachel? wherefore then hast thou beguiled me? And Laban said, It must not be*

*so done in our country, to give the younger before the firstborn. Fulfil her week, and we will give thee this also for the service which thou shalt serve with me yet seven other years. And Jacob did so, and fulfilled her week: and he gave him Rachel his daughter to wife also.*

In Hosea, we see the story of a man who bought his estranged wife from a slave auction after a lifetime of unfaithfulness. Hosea's unthinkable act of selfless love is a window into God's unending love for us.

**Hosea 3:1-3**
*Then said the LORD unto me, Go yet, love a woman beloved of her friend, yet an adulteress, according to the love of the LORD toward the children of Israel, who look to other gods, and love flagons of wine. So I bought her to me for fifteen pieces of silver, and for an homer of barley, and an half homer of barley: And I said unto her, Thou shalt abide for me many days; thou shalt not play the harlot, and thou shalt not be for another man: so will I also be for thee.*

Throughout the Scriptures, we see God's love for man told in heart-wrenching stories of love, betrayal, and redemption. God loves you! The Gospel is the most beautiful love story ever told! There are no words to convey the breadth, depth, and height of God's boundless love for us.

## 2. The Beauty of Salvation's Sacrifice

How can you prove your love for someone? Are loving words the height of commitment? Although we should speak kindly and lovingly to one another, words can be empty. True love is shown through sacrifice. Parents get up every day and go to work when they do not feel like it so that they can take care of their children. Mothers change diapers and make meals no matter how they feel because they love their babies. Husbands and wives stay together when things are difficult because they are committed to one another, and they will sacrifice to prove it. Jesus told us that the greatest love one can express for another is to lay down his own life to save the other.

**John 15:13**
*Greater love hath no man than this, that a man lay down his life for his friends.*

Would you die for anyone? Jesus Christ gave His life so that we can be saved. There is no greater love!

**Romans 5:6–11**
*For when we were yet without strength, in due time Christ died for the ungodly. For scarcely for a righteous man will one die: yet peradventure for a good man some would even dare to die. But God commendeth his love toward us, in that, while we were yet sinners, Christ died for us. Much more then, being now justified by his blood, we shall be saved from wrath through him. For if, when we were enemies, we were reconciled to God by the death of his Son, much more, being reconciled, we shall be saved by his life. And not only so, but we also joy in God through our Lord Jesus Christ, by whom we have now received the atonement.*

God sent His Son Jesus to die for you. He did not die for you because you were good. He died for you because you were a sinner and He wanted to save you. Nobody loves you like Jesus loves you. No one will ever love you as much as God loves you. It is impossible to describe the love of God. It is beautiful.

### 3. The Beauty of Salvation's Succession

Salvation is the beginning of eternal life. God has amazing things planned for your future. Any story of sacrifice is moving. Salvation takes this beauty to a different level.

How can it be that the Almighty God would love sinners such as us? Why would our perfect Creator condescend to love us so? Would you die to save a gnat? Would you give your most precious possession to rescue a mosquito? We are less than a gnat compared to God. We

# THE BEAUTY OF SALVATION

are lower than a mosquito in relation to the Almighty, yet the God of all Glory gave Himself for us! How could it be that the Almighty God would love us so? The hymn entitled "How Can It Be?" asks this age-old question.

> O Savior, as my eyes behold
> The wonders of Thy might untold
> The heav'ns in glorious light arrayed,
> The vast creation Thou hast made—
> And yet to think Thou lovest me—
> My heart cries out, "How can it be?"
>
> As at the cross I humbly bow
> And gaze upon Thy thorn-crowned brow,
> And view the precious bleeding form
> By cruel nails so bruised and torn,
> To know Thy suff'ring was for me,
> In grief I cry, "How can it be?"
>
> How can it be? How can it be?
> Was ever grace so full and free!
> From heights of bliss to depths of woe
> In loving kindness Thou didst go,
> From sin and shame to rescue me—
> O Love Divine, How can it be?
>
> Refrain:
> How can it be? How can it be?
> That God should love a soul like me,
> O how can it be?

Jesus Christ died not only to save us but also to give us incredible gifts along with salvation. Thank God for the benefits of His salvation as you read a few of them below.

- **Heaven:** Christ saved us from Hell, but He did not stop with saving us from eternal damnation. He is making a home for us in Heaven.

**John 14:1–3**
*Let not your heart be troubled: ye believe in God, believe also in me. In my Father's house are many mansions: if it were not so, I would have told you. I go to prepare a place for you. And if I go and prepare a place for you, I will come again, and receive you unto myself; that where I am, there ye may be also.*

Do you see the love of God in these verses? As a bridegroom prepares a home for his bride, our Lord prepares an eternal home for you. He wants to be with you forever.

- **Family:** God did not save us to make us lowly servants. He redeemed us to be His children!

**Romans 8:14–16**
*For as many as are led by the Spirit of God, they are the sons of God. For ye have not received the spirit of bondage again to fear; but ye have received the Spirit of adoption, whereby we cry, Abba, Father. The Spirit itself beareth witness with our spirit, that we are the children of God:*

The word *Abba* is an intimate name like Daddy or Papa. You can go to God as your spiritual Daddy. You can crawl up into His lap to lean upon His everlasting arms.

- **Inheritance:** We are the children of God through faith in the finished work of Jesus Christ. You are not the unloved stepchild of the family of God. You are a joint heir with Christ!

**Romans 8:17**
*And if children, then heirs; heirs of God, and joint-heirs with Christ; if so be that we suffer with him, that we may be also glorified together.*

God has bequeathed you an eternal inheritance. You are a joint heir with the only begotten Son of God. Amazing! You may be poor here on Earth, but you are rich, my Friend. Your Father is the KING of ALL, and you are royalty! Only God Himself could conceive such a beautiful story of salvation.

## 4. The Beauty of Salvation's Doctrines

God describes the elements of salvation with powerful symbols and metaphors. These doctrines express God's unending love and inconceivable sacrifice in moving ways.

- Conception
- Adoption
- Regeneration
- Remission
- Redemption
- Reconciliation
- Propitiation
- Imputation
- Justification
- Sanctification
- Glorification

The rest of this book will explore each of these doctrines. God's plan of salvation is so simple that a child can believe it yet so complex that we can study it for a lifetime only to scratch the surface. While we revel in the theological perfection of the doctrines of grace, let us never forget the beauty of salvation. As you read this simple book, I pray that you will be captivated by salvation's beauty once again. Marvel that God loves you!

## Chapter Two

# The Beauty of Conception

Salvation is beautiful. God describes salvation in various ways throughout the Scriptures to teach us the depth, breadth, and height of His unspeakable gift of eternal life. In this chapter, we will discuss the most well-known illustration of salvation—the new birth. We will use the word *conception* since it illustrates the beauty of the doctrine of the new birth. Our Lord Jesus explained that the new birth is necessary to go to Heaven.

**John 3:5**
*Jesus answered, Verily, verily, I say unto thee, Except a man be born of water and of the Spirit, he cannot enter into the kingdom of God.*

Have you been born again? If so, one of the many benefits of salvation is that God becomes our Heavenly Father. The name "Heavenly Father" is used six times in the New Testament. Jesus taught us to pray to our Heavenly Father.

**Luke 11:1-2**
*And it came to pass, that, as he was praying in a certain place, when he ceased, one of his disciples said unto him, Lord, teach us to pray, as John also taught his disciples. And he said unto them, When ye pray, say, Our Father which art in heaven, Hallowed be thy name. Thy kingdom come. Thy will be done, as in heaven, so in earth.*

The doctrine of the Fatherhood of God continues in verse 13.

**Luke 11:13**
*If ye then, being evil, know how to give good gifts unto your children: how much more shall your heavenly Father give the Holy Spirit to them that ask him?*

Consider the same idea conveyed in Matthew 6.

**Matthew 6:26**
*Behold the fowls of the air: for they sow not, neither do they reap, nor gather into barns; yet your heavenly Father feedeth them. Are ye not much better than they?*

There is only one way we can be privileged to call God our Father. Through saving faith in Jesus Christ, we are born again into the family of God. Meditate upon the multi-faceted beauty of the doctrine of conception.

### Consider the Beauty of Conception's Creation.

Is there anything more beautiful than the birth of a baby? At conception, a new life springs from nothing. Simple cells combine to form a living soul! Then, a tiny body forms by the miracle of creation. Eventually, that small body becomes an adult. Psalm 139 reveals the miraculous workings of God in the womb.

**Psalm 139:13–16**
*For thou hast possessed my reins: thou hast covered me in my mother's womb. I will praise thee; for I am fearfully and wonderfully made: marvellous are thy works; and that my soul knoweth right well. My substance was not hid from thee, when I was made in secret, and curiously wrought in the lowest parts of the earth. Thine eyes did see my substance, yet being unperfect; and in thy book all my members were written, which in continuance were fashioned, when as yet there was none of them.*

# THE BEAUTY OF CONCEPTION

When you put your faith in Christ, you were born into the family of God. At that moment, your soul was created anew in the image of God. You were spiritually conceived as a new creature.

**II Corinthians 5:17**
*Therefore if any man be in Christ, he is a new creature: old things are passed away; behold, all things are become new.*

## Consider the Beauty of Conception's Relation.

When a baby is born, that new life joins a family. A mother visited the edge of death to bring forth life. A happy father awaits to greet the little one from the womb. Grandparents, brothers, sisters, aunts, uncles, and cousins rejoice because of the arrival of the little one in the family.

In His wisdom, the Creator gave us the blessing of being part of a family. Consider the immeasurable love of a mother. Ponder the limitless care of a father. Contemplate the countless meals, the innumerable talks, the incalculable support, and the immeasurable sacrifice that take place over the course of the child's life. Thank God for family! In an act of unthinkable grace, the God of Heaven places those who are born again into His family. We have all the rights and privileges of the children of God.

**Romans 8:16–17**
*The Spirit itself beareth witness with our spirit, that we are the children of God: And if children, then heirs; heirs of God, and joint-heirs with Christ; if so be that we suffer with him, that we may be also glorified together.*

He protects us and provides for us as a loving Father. He supplies all of our needs and protects us from harm. He gives generously and enjoys doting on His children. Furthermore, we have access to the Almighty in unprecedented ways. We are more than subjects. We are His children! We are allowed to approach Him as we do because He is our Father.

We have unlimited access to God. I appreciate my neighbor's children. I would help them in any way I could, but my children have greater access to me than anyone else's children. I see them in the morning, and I put them to bed at night. They are always on my mind. They can call any time, night or day, and I will be there for them. I love to wrap them in my arms and tell them how much I love them. How much greater is our Heavenly Father's love for us! He is a far greater Dad than any human. We are part of the family of God!

**Consider the Beauty of Conception's Duration.**

When a child is born, a new relationship begins that will endure throughout this life. Once a child enters his parents' world, the parents are changed for ever. One person said, "Having a child is like living with your heart outside of your chest for the rest of your life." I have witnessed 90-year-old mothers worry for their 70-year-old children. The love of a parent for a child is a special love that endures the tests of time.

At spiritual conception, you become the child of God. This is an unbreakable bond for all of eternity. Eternal life begins at the moment of salvation. You will be God's child forever. The Fatherhood of God is one of the greatest proofs of eternal security. When your children do wrong, do you start a raging fire in your backyard and throw your children into it? Of course not! You would lovingly discipline them and train them. You are not a more loving parent than God. He will not discard His disobedient children into Hell. Rather, He promises to chastise us for our own good.

Our God chose the family relationship to teach us about our relationship with Him. How thrilling to be God's child through the new birth! Consider a few more aspects of the beauty of conception.

**Consider the Beauty of Unmatched Love.**

God loves us like no one has ever loved us. No one will ever love you as much as God does. He proved His love for you through unthinkable sacrifice. If you ever doubt God's love, simply look to the Cross. Truly, there is no greater love.

**John 3:16**
*For God so loved the world, that he gave his only begotten Son, that whosoever believeth in him should not perish, but have everlasting life.*

### Consider the Beauty of Undeniable Resemblance.

Children tend to look like their parents or grandparents. We take on the attributes of our family. Our Lord Jesus explained that sinners resemble the Devil.

**John 8:44**
*Ye are of your father the devil, and the lusts of your father ye will do. He was a murderer from the beginning, and abode not in the truth, because there is no truth in him. When he speaketh a lie, he speaketh of his own: for he is a liar, and the father of it.*

Scripture explains that the saved should resemble their Heavenly Father. Every family has behaviors and idiosyncrasies. We should strive to be like our Father in spirit, motive, appearance, and manner.

**I Peter 1:16**
*Because it is written, Be ye holy; for I am holy.*

One of these days, we will be glorified and made into the image of Christ. Until then, we should strive to be like Jesus in word and deed.

**I John 3:1-3**
*Behold, what manner of love the Father hath bestowed upon us, that we should be called the sons of God: therefore the world knoweth us not, because it knew him not. Beloved, now are we the sons of God, and it doth not yet appear what we shall be: but we know that, when he shall*

*appear, we shall be like him; for we shall see him as he is. And every man that hath this hope in him purifieth himself, even as he is pure.*

### Consider the Beauty of an Unbreakable Bond.

We can rest in the unbreakable bond of our Father/child relationship with God. Our salvation is as sure as the promises of God.

**John 6:37**
*All that the Father giveth me shall come to me; and him that cometh to me I will in no wise cast out.*

**How can you be born into God's family?**
You have seen all of these tremendous benefits of being God's child. Make sure that you have been born again so that you can reap the benefits.

**John 1:12–13**
*But as many as received him, to them gave he power to become the sons of God, even to them that believe on his name: Which were born, not of blood, nor of the will of the flesh, nor of the will of man, but of God.*

Without Christ, everyone is a sinner headed for eternal judgment. As sinners by birth and by choice, we are lost. The wrath of God abides upon the lost. Our only hope is forgiveness found through personal faith in the death, burial, and resurrection of Jesus Christ. John 1:12 explains two requirements of saving faith.

### 1. We must believe in Christ.

Faith is the currency of God's Kingdom. Salvation is offered to those who believe in the Gospel of Jesus Christ.

**John 11:25–26**
*Jesus said unto her, I am the resurrection, and the life: he that believeth in me, though he were dead, yet shall he live: And whosoever liveth and believeth in me shall never die. Believest thou this?*

# THE BEAUTY OF CONCEPTION

This belief referred to in these verses is more than an acknowledgement of the facts. The devils believe the facts about Christ, but they are not redeemed.

**James 2:19**
*Thou believest that there is one God; thou doest well: the devils also believe, and tremble.*

Saving faith is reliance upon the gift of God.

**Ephesians 2:8-9**
*For by grace are ye saved through faith; and that not of yourselves: it is the gift of God: Not of works, lest any man should boast.*

Jesus died on the Cross to pay for our sins. He offers forgiveness and salvation as a gift to those who believe. Saving faith is more than a mental assent to the historical facts of Christ. It is a heart belief. Salvation comes when you are willing to confess that Christ is exactly Who He claimed to be and to believe in your heart that God raised Him from the dead. If you believe in the resurrection, you are professing faith in His vicarious death and physical burial by default. From what else would He be raised?

**Romans 10:9-10**
*That if thou shalt confess with thy mouth the Lord Jesus, and shalt believe in thine heart that God hath raised him from the dead, thou shalt be saved. For with the heart man believeth unto righteousness; and with the mouth confession is made unto salvation.*

### 2. We must receive Christ.

We not only must believe in the Person and work of Christ but also must receive Him for ourselves. It is not enough for Jesus to be THE Saviour. Saving faith claims Jesus Christ as YOUR Saviour. You can stand at the gate in the airport believing that the plane can get you to your desired destination. However, if you do not get on the plane, that

## THE BEAUTY OF SALVATION

kind of faith will not help you. You must believe that Christ is Who He claims to be and that He has made the way of salvation. Ask yourself the following questions:

- Have you accepted Christ as your personal Saviour?
- Have you been conceived by faith?
- Is God your Heavenly Father?

Choose to accept Christ today! Why not be born again into the family of God right now? Confess that Jesus Christ is the Son of God Who died on the Cross to pay for the sins of the world. Place your faith in His death, burial, and resurrection for the forgiveness of sins. Claim His promise of salvation. Believe in your heart that God raised Him from the dead. Accept Him as your personal Saviour right now.

Why not pray this prayer of salvation while believing in Christ with all of your heart?

*Dear Jesus, I confess that I am a sinner and I can't go to Heaven without You. I don't want to go to Hell. I believe You are the Son of God Who died on the Cross to pay for my sin, was buried, and rose again from the dead. Please forgive all my sin and take me to Heaven when I die. I am trusting You alone as my Saviour. Thank You for saving me. Amen.*

Marvel at God's unspeakable gift. No wonder God chose this beautiful Father/child relationship to teach us about salvation. There is no greater symbol of love, acceptance, and relationship. Strive to be a good child. Rest in the undying love of your Eternal Father. Revel in the beauty of your salvation. Worship God for His goodness and grace!

## Chapter Three

# The Beauty of Adoption

In the last chapter, we discussed the beautiful doctrine of conception. It focuses on our unbreakable family connection with God. In this chapter, we highlight the beautiful doctrine of adoption. It emphasizes the truth that God chose us. You cannot choose a natural-born child. You cannot manipulate the gender, hair color, or personality. God decides who is placed in a family through natural birth.

Adoption is different. Adoption takes place when a loving family chooses to bring an orphan into their family. It is a commitment to accept a stranger with loving arms, provide for his needs, and treat him as a natural-born member of the family.

Do you know a family who adopted a child? Have you known someone who was adopted? Perhaps you were adopted yourself. Adoption is a beautiful thing. It is a godsend for married couples who cannot have a child naturally. Also, it is a tremendous blessing for couples who want more children. More Christians should consider adoption as an option for their families.

The Bible doctrine of adoption is a beautiful illustration of God's love for us in salvation. Webster's 1828 *American Dictionary of the English Language* covers the practical and theological applications of adoption.

Adoption
ADOP'TION, *n.* [L. *adoptio.*]
1. The act of adopting, or the state of being adopted; the taking and treating of a stranger as one's own child.

2. The receiving as one's own, what is new or not natural.
3. God's taking the sinful children of men into his favor and protection. Eph. iv.

*The Baker Encyclopedia of the Bible* offers this definition for adoption.
Adoption
> Theologically, the act of God by which believers become members of "God's family" with all the privileges and obligations of family membership.

*The Holman Illustrated Bible Dictionary* defines adoption in this way.
Adoption
1. Legal process whereby one person receives another into his family and confers upon that person familial privileges and advantages. The "adopter" assumes parental responsibility for the "adoptee." The "adoptee" is thereby considered an actual child, becoming the beneficiary of all the rights, privileges, and responsibilities afforded to all the children of the family.

References to the doctrine of adoption in the Old Testament are rare, but implications can be found. Paul reveals that God adopted the Israelites.

**Romans 9:4**
*Who are Israelites; to whom pertaineth the adoption, and the glory, and the covenants, and the giving of the law, and the service of God, and the promises;*

God chose the Israelites and treated them as a loving Father would treat His children.

**Exodus 4:22**
*And thou shalt say unto Pharaoh, Thus saith the LORD, Israel is my son, even my firstborn:*

**Deuteronomy 32:6**
*Do ye thus requite the LORD, O foolish people and unwise? is not he thy father that hath bought thee? hath he not made thee, and established thee?*

**Isaiah 1:2**
*Hear, O heavens, and give ear, O earth: for the LORD hath spoken, I have nourished and brought up children, and they have rebelled against me.*

**Hosea 11:1**
*When Israel was a child, then I loved him, and called my son out of Egypt.*

The New Testament explanations of the doctrine of adoption are thorough and beautiful. Ponder these Bible truths as we explore the doctrine of adoption.

### 1. Humans are lost and dying in a dysfunctional family.

Before salvation, we are children of the Devil.

**John 8:44**
*Ye are of your father the devil, and the lusts of your father ye will do. He was a murderer from the beginning, and abode not in the truth, because there is no truth in him. When he speaketh a lie, he speaketh of his own: for he is a liar, and the father of it.*

Those without Christ have an abusive spiritual father. Think of the worst situations of parental abuse possible: neglect; physical, mental, emotional, and sexual abuse; endangerment. Satan abuses his children with all these and much more. In the end, the Devil orphans his children, knowing that they will spend eternity in the torments of Hell. The Scriptures explain that the eternal penalty of Satan's sin was conferred upon us when Adam and Eve chose to sin.

**Romans 5:12**
*Wherefore, as by one man sin entered into the world, and death by sin; and so death passed upon all men, for that all have sinned:*

**Ephesians 2:3**
*Among whom also we all had our conversation in times past in the lusts of our flesh, fulfilling the desires of the flesh and of the mind; and were by nature the children of wrath, even as others.*

**Matthew 25:41**
*Then shall he say also unto them on the left hand, Depart from me, ye cursed, into everlasting fire, prepared for the devil and his angels:*

**2. God chooses to love us and offers us a place in His family through faith in Christ.**

Imagine a wealthy couple visiting an orphanage in Russia. Their hearts break as they see bed after bed filled with crying infants who have no one to love them. The children have no money or possessions to offer. Moved with love, the couple spends untold dollars in an effort to bring a child home and love him forever.

Similarly, our Heavenly Father saw us in our abused and orphaned state. He chose to love us when we had nothing to offer Him. He paid an astounding price to purchase our liberty and make us a part of His family.

**John 3:16**
*For God so loved the world, that he gave his only begotten Son, that whosoever believeth in him should not perish, but have everlasting life.*

**Romans 5:8**
*But God commendeth his love toward us, in that, while we were yet sinners, Christ died for us.*

**Ephesians 1:4–6**
*According as he hath chosen us in him before the foundation of the world, that we should be holy and without blame before him in love: Having predestinated us unto the adoption of children by Jesus Christ to himself, according to the good pleasure of his will, To the praise of the glory of his grace, wherein he hath made us accepted in the beloved.*

# THE BEAUTY OF ADOPTION

Spiritual adoption is secured through faith in the Gospel. The personal acceptance of Jesus Christ as the Saviour Who is the Son of God and the belief in His death, burial, and resurrection is the only way of salvation. Through faith in Christ, we are ...*accepted in the beloved.*

**Ephesians 1:6-7**
*To the praise of the glory of his grace, wherein he hath made us accepted in the beloved. In whom we have redemption through his blood, the forgiveness of sins, according to the riches of his grace;*

By faith in Christ, we are redeemed and receive the adoption of sons.

**Galatians 3:7**
*Know ye therefore that they which are of faith, the same are the children of Abraham.*

**Galatians 4:4-5**
*But when the fulness of the time was come, God sent forth his Son, made of a woman, made under the law, To redeem them that were under the law, that we might receive the adoption of sons.*

**3. Adoption gives us all the rights and privileges of a biological child.**

The law sees no difference between a biological child and an adopted child. Likewise, God makes no distinction between the adopted and the conceived. Marvel at the privileges of God's adopted children.

- **Leading of the Father**

**Romans 8:14**
*For as many as are led by the Spirit of God, they are the sons of God.*

- **Security in the Father**

**Romans 8:15**
*For ye have not received the spirit of bondage again to fear; but ye have received the Spirit of adoption, whereby we cry, Abba, Father.*

- **Access to the Father**

**Romans 8:15**
*For ye have not received the spirit of bondage again to fear; but ye have received the Spirit of adoption, whereby we cry, Abba, Father.*

- **Confirmation of Relation**

**Romans 8:16**
*The Spirit itself beareth witness with our spirit, that we are the children of God:*

- **Inheritance of Riches**

**Romans 8:17**
*And if children, then heirs; heirs of God, and joint-heirs with Christ; if so be that we suffer with him, that we may be also glorified together.*

- **Expectation of Deliverance**

**Romans 8:19**
*For the earnest expectation of the creature waiteth for the manifestation of the sons of God.*

- **Glorious Liberty**

**Romans 8:21**
*Because the creature itself also shall be delivered from the bondage of corruption into the glorious liberty of the children of God.*

Every child of God through faith in Christ enjoys all the rights and privileges of a child of God. When was the last time you were moved to tears by the goodness of God? Why not take a few moments right now to thank God for His amazing gifts?

### 4. Believers are two-fold the children of God.

We have two unbreakable bonds with our Heavenly Father. We are children once through conception, the new birth. This speaks of the undeniable bond of a biological connection.

We are children a second time through adoption. This speaks of God's choice. He chose you. He picked you out of the crowd. He decided to love you in spite of all of your flaws, faults, and failures. He knew what He was getting into when He adopted you, but He chose you anyway! Conception and adoption are not competing truths. They work together to show multiple dimensions of our glorious salvation.

### 5. Adoption proves the security of our salvation.

The illustration of adoption in the New Testament has its root in Roman law. Jews did not have a law for adoption. If a man died, his brother automatically would become the head of his household. There was no need for the concept of adoption in Jewish society. Notice that the doctrine of adoption is examined thoroughly in the book of Romans. Adoption had a powerful meaning in Roman culture. Adoption meant:
- The parents freely chose the child, ensuring he was desired by the parents.
- The adopted child received a new identity.
- Any prior commitments, responsibilities, or debts of the adopted child were erased.
- An adopted child could not be disowned by the adoptive parents. The child became a permanent part of the family.

Can you see this amazing truth? God will never disown His adopted children. It is unlawful according to the rules of adoption. Our eternal security is sure through faith in Christ!

**Hebrews 7:25**
*Wherefore he is able also to save them to the uttermost that come unto God by him, seeing he ever liveth to make intercession for them.*

Adopting parents choose a child with no biological connection or legal responsibility and determine to make him or her a part of the family. In similar fashion, God chose to adopt you into His family through faith in the finished work of Jesus Christ. This fact makes believers the two-fold children of God. We are children by birth and by adoption. God saved you to spend eternity with you. He sacrificed Himself to secure your salvation. He is not looking for a reason to get rid of you. Rejoice in the fullness of salvation and in the beauty of adoption!

## Chapter Four

# The Beauty of Redemption

Redemption is a prominent doctrine in God's Word. Learn how much God loves you by investigating this powerful precept. The word *redemption* is found 20 times in the King James Bible. The word *redeem* occurs 139 times. The word *redemption* comes from the word *redeem*. *Redeem* means "to buy back."

Webster's 1828 *American Dictionary of the English Language* provides a multi-faceted definition of the word.

Redeem
REDEE'M, *v. t.* [L. *redimo; red, re,* and *emo,* to obtain or purchase.]
1. To purchase back; to ransom; to liberate or rescue from captivity or bondage, or from any obligation or liability to suffer or to be forfeited, by paying an equivalent; as, to *redeem* prisoners or captured goods; to *redeem* a pledge.
2. To repurcha se what has been sold; to regain possession of a thing alienated, by repaying the value of it to the possessor.
    If a man [shall] sell a dwelling house in a walled city, then he may *redeem* it within a whole year after it is sold. Levi. xxv.
3. To rescue; to recover; to deliver from.
    Th' Almighty from the grave hath me *redeem'd*.   Sandys
    *Redeem* Israel, O God, out of all his troubles. Ps. xxv. Deut. vii.
    The mass of earth not yet *redeemed* from chaos.   S. S. Smith
4. To compensate; to make amends for.
    It is a chance which does *redeem* all sorrows.   Shak

> By lesser ills the greater to *redeem*.     *Dryden*

5. To free by making atonement.
   > Thou hast one daughter
   > Who *redeems* nature from the general curse.     *Shak*
6. To pay the penalty of.
   > Which of you will be mortal to *redeem* Man's mortal crime?
   >     *Milton*
7. To save.
   > He could not have *redeemed* a portion of his time for contemplating the powers of nature.     *S. S. Smith*
8. To perform what has been promised; to make good by performance. He has *redeemed* his pledge or promise.
9. In *law*, to recall an estate, or to obtain the right to re-enter upon a mortgaged estate by paying to the mortgagee his principal, interest, and expenses or costs.     *Blackstone*
10. In *theology*, to rescue and deliver from the bondage of sin and the penalties of God's violated law, by obedience and suffering in the place of the sinner, or by doing and suffering that which is accepted in lieu of the sinner's obedience.
    > Christ hath *redeemed* us from the curse of the law, being made a curse for us. Gal. iii. Tit.ii..

Now consider Webster's definition of the word *redemption*.

Redemption
REDEMP'TION, *n.* [Fr.; It. *redenzione*; Sp. *redencion;* from L. *redemptio*. See *Redeem*.]
1. Repurchase of captured goods or prisoners; the act of procuring the deliverance of persons or things from the possession and power of captors by the payment of an equivalent; ransom; release; as the *redemption* of prisoners taken in war; the *redemption* of a ship and cargo.
2. Deliverance from bondage, distress, or from liability to any evil or forfeiture, either by money, labor or other means.
3. Repurchase, as of lands alienated. Lev. xxv. Jer. xxxii.

4. The liberation of an estate from a mortgage; or the purchase of the right to re-enter upon it by paying the principal sum for which it was mortgaged, with interest and cost; also, the right of redeeming and re-entering.
5. Repurchase of notes, bills or other evidence of debt by paying their value in specie to their holders.
6. In *theology,* the purchase of God's favor by the death and sufferings of Christ; the ransom or deliverance of sinners from the bondage of sin and the penalties of God's violated law by the atonement of Christ. *Dryden. Nelson.*

In whom we have *redemption* through his blood. Eph. i. Col. i.

Redemption was a familiar theme in Jewish life. A Jew could redeem:

- **Family land that had been sold**

**Leviticus 25:23-24**
*The land shall not be sold for ever: for the land is mine; for ye are strangers and sojourners with me. And in all the land of your possession ye shall grant a redemption for the land.*

- **Possessions**

**Leviticus 25:25**
*If thy brother be waxen poor, and hath sold away some of his possession, and if any of his kin come to redeem it, then shall he redeem that which his brother sold.*

- **A city dwelling**

**Leviticus 25:29**
*And if a man sell a dwelling house in a walled city, then he may redeem it within a whole year after it is sold; within a full year may he redeem it.*

- **An indentured servant**

**Leviticus 25:51**
*If there be yet many years behind, according unto them he shall give again the price of his redemption out of the money that he was bought for.*

In addition, we find that redemption is ingrained into the Hebrews' history with God. Jehovah redeemed the Israelites from Egypt. The Lord made the promise of redemption.

**Exodus 6:6**
*Wherefore say unto the children of Israel, I am the LORD, and I will bring you out from under the burdens of the Egyptians, and I will rid you out of their bondage, and I will redeem you with a stretched out arm, and with great judgments:*

In Moses' song of victory after the exodus from Egypt, the fulfillment of Jehovah's promise was praised.

**Exodus 15:13**
*Thou in thy mercy hast led forth the people which thou hast redeemed: thou hast guided them in thy strength unto thy holy habitation.*

Salvation is a story of redemption. Many Bible verses speak of spiritual redemption. Here are a few.

**Psalm 49:8**
*(For the redemption of their soul is precious, and it ceaseth for ever:)*

**Psalm 111:9**
*He sent redemption unto his people: he hath commanded his covenant for ever: holy and reverend is his name.*

**Psalm 130:7**
*Let Israel hope in the LORD: for with the LORD there is mercy, and with him is plenteous redemption.*

# THE BEAUTY OF REDEMPTION

We need redemption because of sin. When Adam sinned, he plunged the entire human race into sin and destruction.

**Romans 5:12**
*Wherefore, as by one man sin entered into the world, and death by sin; and so death passed upon all men, for that all have sinned:*

The penalty of Lucifer's rebellion was passed onto mankind.

**Matthew 25:41**
*Then shall he say also unto them on the left hand, Depart from me, ye cursed, into everlasting fire, prepared for the devil and his angels:*

The dominion that God gave Adam in the garden transferred to the Devil.

**Genesis 1:28**
*And God blessed them, and God said unto them, Be fruitful, and multiply, and replenish the earth, and subdue it: and have dominion over the fish of the sea, and over the fowl of the air, and over every living thing that moveth upon the earth.*

**II Corinthians 4:4**
*In whom the god of this world hath blinded the minds of them which believe not, lest the light of the glorious gospel of Christ, who is the image of God, should shine unto them.*

The Gospel of Christ bought us back from sin and death! Jesus Christ died to pay for our sin.

**Romans 5:8**
*But God commendeth his love toward us, in that, while we were yet sinners, Christ died for us.*

**II Corinthians 5:21**
*For he hath made him to be sin for us, who knew no sin; that we might be made the righteousness of God in him.*

Through redemption, we no longer are slaves to sin.

**Romans 6:17–18**
*But God be thanked, that ye were the servants of sin, but ye have obeyed from the heart that form of doctrine which was delivered you. Being then made free from sin, ye became the servants of righteousness.*

Creation is redeemed as well and awaits deliverance.

**Romans 8:21–23**
*Because the creature itself also shall be delivered from the bondage of corruption into the glorious liberty of the children of God. For we know that the whole creation groaneth and travaileth in pain together until now. And not only they, but ourselves also, which have the firstfruits of the Spirit, even we ourselves groan within ourselves, waiting for the adoption, to wit, the redemption of our body.*

Redemption is granted through personal faith in Jesus Christ.

**Romans 3:24**
*Being justified freely by his grace through the redemption that is in Christ Jesus:*

**I Corinthians 1:30**
*But of him are ye in Christ Jesus, who of God is made unto us wisdom, and righteousness, and sanctification, and redemption:*

**Ephesians 1:7**
*In whom we have redemption through his blood, the forgiveness of sins, according to the riches of his grace;*

**Colossians 1:14**
*In whom we have redemption through his blood, even the forgiveness of sins:*

# THE BEAUTY OF REDEMPTION

**Hebrews 9:12**
*Neither by the blood of goats and calves, but by his own blood he entered in once into the holy place, having obtained eternal redemption for us.*

## Redemption and the Example of Hosea

The story of Hosea and Gomer pictures the beautiful doctrine of redemption. Follow these facts as the story unfolds.
- Hosea married a harlot.
- Hosea and Gomer had three children.
- Gomer left the family to pursue her lovers.
- Hosea remained faithful.
- After many years, Hosea saw his unfaithful wife, Gomer, on the selling block of a slave market.
- Hosea sold all he had so he could buy Gomer and bring her home.

**Hosea 3:2**
*So I bought her to me for fifteen pieces of silver, and for an homer of barley, and an half homer of barley:*

INCREDIBLE! Would your love stand this test? The account of Hosea and Gomer illustrates our unfaithfulness to God and His unwavering love and amazing sacrifice for us. Consider the facts of our redemption.
- God created us to be His.
- We left Him to pursue sin and pleasure.
- God loves us in spite of our unfaithfulness.
- He bought us off the sinner's slave block.
- He redeemed us from a life of debt and slavery of sin to make us His own once more.

We have been redeemed! ASTONISHING! Such love is too wonderful to understand! Nevertheless, we experience it through the beautiful doctrine of redemption.

# THE BEAUTY OF SALVATION

## RANSOM is a similar theme to redemption.

What is a ransom? Webster's 1828 Dictionary offers this illustrative definition.

Ransom
RAN'SŎM, *n.* [Dan. *ranzon;* Sw. *ranson;* G. *ranzion;* Norm. *raancon;* Fr. *rançon;* Arm. *rançzon. In French, the word implies not only redemption, but exaction; but I know not the component parts of the word. Qu. G. sühne,* atonement.]
1. The money or price paid for the redemption of a prisoner or slave, or for goods captured by an enemy; that which procures the release of a prisoner or captive, or of captured property, and restores the one to liberty and the other to the original owner.
    By his captivity in Austria, and the heavy *ransom* he paid for his liberty, Richard was hindered from pursuing the conquest of Ireland. *Davies.*
2. Release from captivity, bondage or the possession of an enemy. They were unable to procure the *ransom* of the prisoners.
3. In *law*, a sum paid for the pardon of some great offense and the discharge of the offender; or a fine paid in lieu of corporal punishment. *Encyc. Blackstone.*
4. In *Scripture*, the price paid for a forfeited life, or for delivery or release from capital punishment.
    Then he shall give for the *ransom* of his life, whatever is laid upon him. Ex. xxi.
5. The price paid for procuring the pardon of sins and the redemption of the sinner from punishment.
    Deliver him from going down to the pit; I have found a *ransom*. Job xxxiii.
    The Son of man came—to give his life a *ransom* for many. Matt. xx. Mark 10.

This word is used sixteen times in the King James Bible. Here are two notable examples.

# THE BEAUTY OF REDEMPTION

**Mark 10:45**
*For even the Son of man came not to be ministered unto, but to minister, and to give his life a ransom for many.*

**I Timothy 2:6**
*Who gave himself a ransom for all, to be testified in due time.*

Follow the idea of ransom compared to salvation.
- Mankind was created for God in His image.
- Satan kidnapped Adam and Eve through sin.
- The ransom required was sinless blood.
- Our Lord sacrificed Himself for our deliverance.
- Through faith in Christ, we are returned to our Father!

We have been ransomed! We have been redeemed! Oh, how I love to sing the beautiful hymn "Redeemed!" Praise God in your heart as you read the powerful lyrics.

Redeemed, how I love to proclaim it!
Redeemed by the blood of the Lamb;
Redeemed thru His infinite mercy,
His child, and forever, I am.

Redeemed, and so happy in Jesus,
No language my rapture can tell;
I know that the light of His presence
With me doth continually dwell.

I think of my blessed Redeemer,
I think of Him all the day long;
I sing, for I cannot be silent;
His love is the theme of my song.

I know I shall see in His beauty
The King in whose law I delight;
Who lovingly guardeth my footsteps
And giveth me songs in the night.

# THE BEAUTY OF SALVATION

CHORUS
Redeemed, redeemed,
Redeemed by the blood of the Lamb;
Redeemed, redeemed,
His child, and forever, I am.

Salvation is a beautiful story of redemption. No greater tale of love and sacrifice has ever been told. Jesus Christ bought us back from sin and Hell with His own blood. Will you trust Him today? Will you thank Him right now for His great love and sacrifice?

## Chapter Five

# The Beauty of Regeneration

The doctrine of regeneration demonstrates the beauty of salvation and reveals the depth of change that occurs when you are born again. Learn how regeneration can make your life exponentially better.

**Titus 3:4–7**
*But after that the kindness and love of God our Saviour toward man appeared, Not by works of righteousness which we have done, but according to his mercy he saved us, by the washing of regeneration, and renewing of the Holy Ghost; Which he shed on us abundantly through Jesus Christ our Saviour; That being justified by his grace, we should be made heirs according to the hope of eternal life.*

The word *regeneration* is a Christian term used as a synonym for the words *salvation* and *conversion*. That use is appropriate. However, examining the subtle differences between these words illuminates a beautiful truth about salvation that is often overlooked. Regeneration reinforces the doctrine of conception, the new birth. However, there is an essential difference between the similar doctrines of conception and regeneration. Conception emphasizes the renewed relationship with the Heavenly Father. Regeneration highlights our brand-new nature as His child.

What is regeneration? Ponder this definition found in Webster's 1828 *American Dictionary of the English Language.*

Regeneration
REGENERA'TION, *n.*
1. Reproduction; the act of producing anew.
2. In *theology,* new birth by the grace of God; that change by which the will and natural enmity of man to God and his law are subdued, and a principle of supreme love to God and his law, or holy affections, are implanted in the heart.

> He saved us by the washing of *regeneration* and renewing of the Holy Spirit. Tit. iii.

The word *regeneration* is found two times in Scripture. Each occurrence underscores essential teachings.

### 1. The Regeneration of Creation

**Matthew 19:28**
*And Jesus said unto them, Verily I say unto you, That ye which have followed me, in the regeneration when the Son of man shall sit in the throne of his glory, ye also shall sit upon twelve thrones, judging the twelve tribes of Israel.*

There is coming a day when all of creation will be made new. When mankind sinned, the entire world was corrupted. Every pain, sorrow, and suffering grew from the first sin. Creation was infected and perverted by sin as well. In the beginning, God's creation existed in perfect harmony. The weather was perfect. The animal kingdom lived in peace as the lion laid down with the lamb. Roses did not have thorns. Every day was perfect. After Adam's sin, Creation itself groaned, waiting to be delivered from the terrible penalty of sin.

**Romans 8:19–23**
*For the earnest expectation of the creature waiteth for the manifestation of the sons of God. For the creature was made subject to vanity, not willingly, but by reason of him who hath subjected the same in hope, Because the creature itself also shall be delivered from the bondage of corruption into the glorious liberty of the children of God. For we know*

*that the whole creation groaneth and travaileth in pain together until now. And not only they, but ourselves also, which have the firstfruits of the Spirit, even we ourselves groan within ourselves, waiting for the adoption, to wit, the redemption of our body.*

One day, at the completion of salvation, believers will be glorified, our bodies will be redeemed, and Heaven and Earth will be made new.

**Revelation 21:1**
*And I saw a new heaven and a new earth: for the first heaven and the first earth were passed away; and there was no more sea.*

### 2. The Regeneration of Salvation

The second appearance of the word *regeneration* in the Bible refers to salvation.

### Why do we need regeneration?

We need to be regenerated because of sin!

**Titus 3:3**
*For we ourselves also were sometimes foolish, disobedient, deceived, serving divers lusts and pleasures, living in malice and envy, hateful, and hating one another.*

This list of sins is an appropriate description of sinful man. The word *foolish* means "unintelligent, sensual, and unwise." *Disobedient* means "unpersuadable." People do what they want regardless of what God says. *Deceived* means "to wander out of the way." Sinners are deceived by Satan and their own hearts. The phrase *serving divers lusts and pleasures* speaks of the bondage of wanting the forbidden and seeking pleasure at any cost. Personal relationships are characterized by *malice* (hurting others without cause), *envy* (jealousy at the blessings of others), *hateful*, and *hating one another*.

Wow! What a list! These sins are only a sampling of the transgressions committed by the lost against our spotless God. Every sin is an offense to our Holy God. Each transgression demands eternal judgment. All iniquity carries the penalty of eternal death. Only a complete transformation (regeneration) from sinner to saint can save sinners from everlasting fire.

## How do we receive regeneration?

**Titus 3:4-6**
*But after that the kindness and love of God our Saviour toward man appeared, Not by works of righteousness which we have done, but according to his mercy he saved us, by the washing of regeneration, and renewing of the Holy Ghost; Which he shed on us abundantly through Jesus Christ our Saviour;*

The wages of sin are death and Hell. The only hope of escaping this payment is salvation through the finished work of Jesus Christ! God showed kindness and love toward man when we deserved judgment. Good works can never erase the debt of past sin or protect us from future sins. Through an act of ultimate mercy, God made a way for us to escape eternal death. Through an act of supreme grace, God sent Jesus Christ, His only begotten Son, to die on the Cross of Calvary in our place.

Placing our personal faith in the death, burial, and resurrection of Christ separates us from the penalty of our sin and saves our souls. Regeneration occurs at the moment of salvation.

## What is the beauty of regeneration?

Regeneration reinforces the doctrine of conception, the new birth. There is an essential difference between these similar salvation doctrines. Conception emphasizes the renewed relationship with the Heavenly Father. Regeneration highlights our brand-new nature as His child. Titus 3:5 describes two amazing miracles that happen at the moment of salvation.

- The washing of regeneration
- The renewing of the Holy Ghost

To discover what these miracles are, let us review a foundational fact of salvation. Every sinner must be born again of the Holy Spirit to go to Heaven.

**John 3:3**
*Jesus answered and said unto him, Verily, verily, I say unto thee, Except a man be born again, he cannot see the kingdom of God.*

Nicodemus was perplexed at this decisive pronouncement from the Saviour. Our Lord explained that Nicodemus needed a new birth spiritually.

**John 3:4–6**
*Nicodemus saith unto him, How can a man be born when he is old? can he enter the second time into his mother's womb, and be born? Jesus answered, Verily, verily, I say unto thee, Except a man be born of water and of the Spirit, he cannot enter into the kingdom of God. That which is born of the flesh is flesh; and that which is born of the Spirit is spirit.*

Jesus said that we must be born of water and of the Spirit. These verses link to Titus 3:5 which mentions washing and the Holy Spirit. Some who read the Bible are tempted to assume that every verse mentioning water refers to baptism. That is a big mistake. If you believe every reference to water means baptism, then you will be led to believe that water baptism has saving power. We know from our study of God's Word that baptism is an act of obedience after salvation. It plays no part in saving the soul. Instead, baptism gives us a good conscience toward God as we publicly claim Him as Saviour and commit to follow Him.

**I Peter 3:21**
*The like figure whereunto even baptism doth also now save us (not the putting away of the filth of the flesh, but the answer of a good conscience toward God,) by the resurrection of Jesus Christ:*

The word *water* in John 3:4 refers to the Word of God. How do we know that? Water is a symbol of the Word of God in Scripture. The washing of regeneration in Titus 3:5 speaks of water. The Greek word for *washing* in this verse is found only one other time in Scripture.

**Ephesians 5:26**
*That he might sanctify and cleanse it with the washing of water by the word,*

This verse speaks of the washing power of God's Word. The Bible is a cleansing agent!

**Psalm 119:9**
*Wherewithal shall a young man cleanse his way? by taking heed thereto according to thy word.*

**The Word of God is a necessary element in the new birth.**

**Romans 10:13–15**
*For whosoever shall call upon the name of the Lord shall be saved. How then shall they call on him in whom they have not believed? and how shall they believe in him of whom they have not heard? and how shall they hear without a preacher? And how shall they preach, except they be sent? as it is written, How beautiful are the feet of them that preach the gospel of peace, and bring glad tidings of good things!*

We are born again to a living hope! The same power that raised Jesus Christ from the dead, works in the sinner to raise his dead spirit and give new life and to birth him into the family of God.

**I Peter 1:3**
*Blessed be the God and Father of our Lord Jesus Christ, which according to his abundant mercy hath begotten us again unto a lively hope by the resurrection of Jesus Christ from the dead,*

# THE BEAUTY OF REGENERATION

We are born again by the Holy Spirit and by God's Holy Word. The Word is the seed, and the Spirit gives it life within us.

**I Peter 1:23**
*Being born again, not of corruptible seed, but of incorruptible, by the word of God, which liveth and abideth for ever.*

Titus 3:5 and John 3:5 teach us that the Word of God and the Spirit of God work together to accomplish the new birth when a sinner receives Jesus Christ as Saviour. The Word of God washes, and the Holy Ghost renews.

There is a final element of regeneration that is truly exciting!

## Re-gened in Jesus

According to *Oxford Dictionary*, a gene is "(in informal use) a unit of heredity which is transferred from a parent to offspring and is held to determine some characteristic of the offspring."

Genes are passed on from parents to children and contain the information to specify traits. A believer in Christ becomes a new creature with a new nature.

**II Corinthians 5:17**
*Therefore if any man be in Christ, he is a new creature: old things are passed away; behold, all things are become new.*

The new nature is eternal like God.

**I John 5:20**
*And we know that the Son of God is come, and hath given us an understanding, that we may know him that is true, and we are in him that is true, even in his Son Jesus Christ. This is the true God, and eternal life.*

The new nature is righteous like God.

**Ephesians 4:22-24**
*That ye put off concerning the former conversation the old man, which is corrupt according to the deceitful lusts; And be renewed in the spirit of your mind; And that ye put on the new man, which after God is created in righteousness and true holiness.*

Like God, the new nature cannot sin.

**I John 3:9**
*Whosoever is born of God doth not commit sin; for his seed remaineth in him: and he cannot sin, because he is born of God.*

This verse has caused some controversy through the ages. Some believe that it teaches that Christians never sin or can reach sinless perfection on Earth. Both of those ideas do not agree with Scripture in its entirety. This verse does not mean that genuine Christians never sin. We know that believers will never be sinless until we are glorified in Heaven.

The meaning of this verse is clear. If one is truly born again, he does not habitually commit sin. He does not make sin his business. It is not the priority of his life. He is no longer a slave to sin. While a Christian can become backslidden for any length of time, he will be chastised by the Saviour. If one can live in constant sin with no conviction or correction, the Bible declares that person to be lost.

Believers can backslide. However, a believer cannot live happily in sin because he has a new nature. God's seed remains in him. That seed is the regenerated part of the Christian. In the New Testament, it is referred to as the "new man." It is righteous and holy and is formed in the image of God. The flesh sins and loves to sin. The regenerated part of the redeemed CANNOT sin.

Our new nature, born after God, is wrapped in this sinful flesh. This results in two warring natures.

**Galatians 5:16-17**
*This I say then, Walk in the Spirit, and ye shall not fulfil the lust of the flesh. For the flesh lusteth against the Spirit, and the Spirit against the*

# THE BEAUTY OF REGENERATION

*flesh: and these are contrary the one to the other: so that ye cannot do the things that ye would.*

As Christians, we must dedicate ourselves to seeking God and living a holy life in constant surrender to the Word and the Spirit. If we allow our flesh to lead, we will become castaways with lives destroyed on the rocky shoals of sin. If we walk in the Spirit, we will be delivered from the earthly consequences of sin, bringing glory to God as we serve Him.

You are a new creature in Christ. You have been washed by the Word and renewed by the Spirit. There is a part of you made in the eternal, sinless image of God. You have been redeemed and re-gened. Regeneration reinforces the doctrine of conception, the new birth, with an important difference. Conception emphasizes the renewed relationship with the Heavenly Father. Regeneration highlights our brand-new nature as His child. Your redeemed soul has been recreated with the eternal nature of our holy God.

## Chapter Six

# The Beauty of Reconciliation

Have you ever had something come between you and a friend or a family member? Think about a time when you had a problem with someone. You did not want to see that person. You did not want to talk to him. When you thought of him, you felt uneasy. You needed reconciliation. What is reconciliation? Let us consult our trusty Webster's 1828 *American Dictionary of the English Language*.

Reconciliation
RECONCILIA'TION, *n.* [Fr. from L. *reconciliatio.*]
1. The act of reconciling parties at variance; renewal of friendship after disagreement or enmity.
   Reconciliation and friendship with God, really form the basis of all rational and true enjoyment. *S. Miller.*
2. In *Scripture,* the means by which sinners are reconciled and brought into a state of favor with God, after natural estrangement or enmity; the atonement; expiation.
   Seventy weeks are determined upon thy people and upon thy holy city, to finish the transgression and to make an end of sin, and to make *reconciliation* for iniquity. Dan. ix. Heb. ii.
3. Agreement of things seemingly opposite, different or inconsistent. *Rogers.*

The word *reconciliation* comes from the word *reconcile.* Let us examine its definition for deeper insight.

Reconcile
RECONCI'LE, *v. t.* [Fr. *reconcilier;* L. *reconcilio; re* and *concilio; con* and *calo,* to *call,* Gr. καλεω. The literal sense is to call back into union.]
1. To conciliate anew; to call back into union and friendship the affections which have been alienated; to restore to friendship or favor after estrangement; as, to *reconcile* men or parties that have been at variance.

    Go thy way; first be *reconciled* to thy brother– Matt. v.
    We pray you in Christ's stead, be ye *reconciled* to God. 2 Cor. v. Eph. ii. Col. i.
2. To bring to acquiescence, content or quiet submission; with *to;* as, to *reconcile* one's self *to* afflictions. It is our duty to be *reconciled to* the dispensations of Providence.
3. To make consistent or congruous; to bring to agreement or suitableness; followed by *with* or *to*.

    The great men among the ancients understood how to *reconcile* manual labor *with* affairs of state.    *Locke.*
    Some figures monstrous and misshap'd appear,
    Considered singly, or beheld too near;
    Which but proportion'd to their light and place,
    Due distance *reconciles to* form and grace.    *Pope.*
4. To adjust; to settle; as, to *reconcile* differences or quarrels.

Reconciliation is necessary in every relationship, including in our relationship with God. Consider these amazing Bible verses.

**II Corinthians 5:18–21**
*And all things are of God, who hath reconciled us to himself by Jesus Christ, and hath given to us the ministry of reconciliation; To wit, that God was in Christ, reconciling the world unto himself, not imputing their trespasses unto them; and hath committed unto us the word of reconciliation. Now then we are ambassadors for Christ, as though God did beseech you by us: we pray you in Christ's stead, be ye reconciled to God. For he hath made him to be sin for us, who knew no sin; that we might be made the righteousness of God in him.*

# THE BEAUTY OF RECONCILIATION

When we were born again, we were reconciled to God. Let us explore the beautiful doctrine of reconciliation.

**1. The Must of Reconciliation**

Reconciliation is necessary because of sin. Sin separates us from God.

**Isaiah 59:1-2**
*Behold, the LORD'S hand is not shortened, that it cannot save; neither his ear heavy, that it cannot hear: But your iniquities have separated between you and your God, and your sins have hid his face from you, that he will not hear.*

Sinners are far off from God. We can only be reconciled to God through the blood of Christ. Consider these powerful verses.

**Ephesians 2:13**
*But now in Christ Jesus ye who sometimes were far off are made nigh by the blood of Christ.*

The lost are strangers and foreigners.

**Ephesians 2:19**
*Now therefore ye are no more strangers and foreigners, but fellowcitizens with the saints, and of the household of God;*

Transgressors are alienated and are enemies.

**Colossians 1:21**
*And you, that were sometime alienated and enemies in your mind by wicked works, yet now hath he reconciled*

The wages of sin is physical death on Earth and spiritual death by spending eternity in Hell.

**Romans 6:23**
*For the wages of sin is death; but the gift of God is eternal life through Jesus Christ our Lord.*

**Revelation 21:8**
*But the fearful, and unbelieving, and the abominable, and murderers, and whoremongers, and sorcerers, and idolaters, and all liars, shall have their part in the lake which burneth with fire and brimstone: which is the second death.*

As long as there is sin between us, man cannot be right with God. **Who can make us right with God?** Job lamented that there was not a DAYSMAN or mediator between him and God.

**Job 9:32–34**
*For he is not a man, as I am, that I should answer him, and we should come together in judgment. Neither is there any daysman betwixt us, that might lay his hand upon us both. Let him take his rod away from me, and let not his fear terrify me:*

### 2. The Man of Reconciliation

Jesus Christ is our Daysman. He is the Mediator between God and man. Christ satisfied God's need for justice by sacrificing Himself to pay for our sins.

**Romans 5:10**
*For if, when we were enemies, we were reconciled to God by the death of his Son, much more, being reconciled, we shall be saved by his life.*

**Hebrews 2:17**
*Wherefore in all things it behoved him to be made like unto his brethren, that he might be a merciful and faithful high priest in things pertaining to God, to make reconciliation for the sins of the people.*

# THE BEAUTY OF RECONCILIATION

**I Timothy 2:5-6**
*For there is one God, and one mediator between God and men, the man Christ Jesus; Who gave himself a ransom for all, to be testified in due time.*

### 3. The Manner of Reconciliation

There must be a way to make things right. Years ago, a lady was causing trouble in the church by spreading lies against me. I called her into my office to reconcile. After a lengthy conversation as I tried to help her, I said, "I sense that you have something against me. How can I make it right?"

She looked at me stone-faced and replied, "You can't."

"That's not Biblical," I answered.

She shrugged her shoulders. Needless to say, she did not stay in the church much longer after that. Her future was sealed when she refused to forgive. Her family spent years struggling spiritually.

Every lasting relationship needs reconciliation to survive. I am thankful God made a way of salvation!

**Ephesians 2:16**
*And that he might reconcile both unto God in one body by the cross, having slain the enmity thereby:*

Jesus died on the Cross to purchase our ransom. When we rely upon the substitutionary death, burial, and resurrection of Christ, we are cleansed from sin and reconciled unto God. Let us look at the verses surrounding the verse above to gain some context.

**Ephesians 2:13-19**
*But now in Christ Jesus ye who sometimes were far off are made nigh by the blood of Christ. For he is our peace, who hath made both one, and hath broken down the middle wall of partition between us; Having abolished in his flesh the enmity, even the law of commandments contained in ordinances; for to make in himself of twain one new man, so making peace; And that he might reconcile both unto God in one body by the*

*cross, having slain the enmity thereby: And came and preached peace to you which were afar off, and to them that were nigh. For through him we both have access by one Spirit unto the Father. Now therefore ye are no more strangers and foreigners, but fellowcitizens with the saints, and of the household of God;*

The blood of Christ is sufficient payment to remove our sin and reconcile us unto the Father.

**Colossians 1:20–22**
*And, having made peace through the blood of his cross, by him to reconcile all things unto himself; by him, I say, whether they be things in earth, or things in heaven. And you, that were sometime alienated and enemies in your mind by wicked works, yet now hath he reconciled in the body of his flesh through death, to present you holy and unblameable and unreproveable in his sight:*

Personal faith in the Person and work of Christ is the manner of salvation. How much God must love us to pay such a high price for our souls!

### 4. The Mandate of Reconciliation

God paid the ultimate price to reconcile us to Himself. He expects us to reconcile with one another when sin comes between us.

**Matthew 5:24**
*Leave there thy gift before the altar, and go thy way; first be reconciled to thy brother, and then come and offer thy gift.*

Jesus taught us that we should be right with our neighbors. Leave your gift. Do not act spiritual if you are not right with your brother or sister. Get it right! Get right vertically with God. Get right horizontally with man. You cannot be wrong with man and right with God. You cannot keep people from being wrong with you, but you can do your part to make things right with others.

## 5. The Ministry of Reconciliation

Believers are drafted to tell sinners that they can be reconciled to God. We call this service evangelism or soulwinning. The Scriptures call it the ministry of reconciliation.

**II Corinthians 5:18–20**
*And all things are of God, who hath reconciled us to himself by Jesus Christ, and hath given to us the ministry of reconciliation; To wit, that God was in Christ, reconciling the world unto himself, not imputing their trespasses unto them; and hath committed unto us the word of reconciliation. Now then we are ambassadors for Christ, as though God did beseech you by us: we pray you in Christ's stead, be ye reconciled to God.*

Are we ever more like Christ when we are trying to reconcile the lost to our Holy God? We become human instruments of mediation. We point the lost to the Great Mediator, to the perfect Reconciler!

We have discussed five important truths in this chapter that illustrate the beauty of the doctrine of reconciliation.

- The must of reconciliation is our urgent need of salvation.
- The Man of reconciliation is Jesus Christ the Saviour.
- The manner of reconciliation is faith in the Gospel.
- The mandate of reconciliation is the command to forgive one another.
- The ministry of reconciliation is the commission to tell sinners that reconciliation with God is available through Jesus Christ.

Have you been reconciled to God through faith in Christ? Have you been reconciled to the people in your life? Are you seeking to reconcile others to God through soulwinning? Praise God for reconciliation available through Christ!

## Chapter Seven

# The Beauty of Remission

The remission of sins is the result of believing the Gospel. Have your sins been remitted? Do you know the depth of God's forgiveness? Discover the beauty of this salvation doctrine.

**Acts 10:42–43**
*And he commanded us to preach unto the people, and to testify that it is he which was ordained of God to be the Judge of quick and dead. To him give all the prophets witness, that through his name whosoever believeth in him shall receive remission of sins.*

The word *remission* is a Bible word that is not used often in our daily language. Its only common reference in our daily vernacular is regarding cancer. How many times have you heard that someone's cancer has "gone into remission?" Remission is a synonym for forgiveness. Let us investigate the deeper meaning of this word to further reveal the beauty of our so great salvation. Acts 10 recounts the incredible story of how a well-known Gentile was saved through faith in Christ.

**Acts 10:1**
*There was a certain man in Caesarea called Cornelius, a centurion of the band called the Italian band,*

Cornelius was an officer in the Roman army. As a centurion, he led one hundred soldiers. The Scripture goes on to tell us that he was a centurion in the band called the Italian band. This was an elite group of soldiers comparable to American Special Forces today. Roman soldiers were known for their ferocity in battle and their meanness on the streets. They went where they wanted and took what they wanted, and no one was able to stop them. They enjoyed vast power and broad immunity in public behavior. Most soldiers used these gifts to their fullest personal benefit and to the hurt of the common citizen. However, Cornelius was different. He as a devout man who feared God with his entire household. He prayed often and gave significant alms.

**Acts 10:2**
*A devout man, and one that feared God with all his house, which gave much alms to the people, and prayed to God alway.*

The Almighty sent an angel to Cornelius telling him to send for the Apostle Peter. Peter would tell him what to do. Cornelius sent two servants and a soldier to ask the apostle to come and preach to them.

**Acts 10:3–8**
*He saw in a vision evidently about the ninth hour of the day an angel of God coming in to him, and saying unto him, Cornelius. And when he looked on him, he was afraid, and said, What is it, Lord? And he said unto him, Thy prayers and thine alms are come up for a memorial before God. And now send men to Joppa, and call for one Simon, whose surname is Peter: He lodgeth with one Simon a tanner, whose house is by the sea side: he shall tell thee what thou oughtest to do. And when the angel which spake unto Cornelius was departed, he called two of his household servants, and a devout soldier of them that waited on him continually; And when he had declared all these things unto them, he sent them to Joppa.*

Immediately, we notice two important facts in this passage.

**1. Cornelius was a good man doing good works with good intentions, but he still needed to be saved by believing the Gospel of Jesus Christ.**

# THE BEAUTY OF REMISSION

Faith in Jesus Christ is the only way of salvation.

**John 14:6**
*Jesus saith unto him, I am the way, the truth, and the life: no man cometh unto the Father, but by me.*

**2. God made sure this sincere but lost man received the Gospel.**

Critics of the Gospel ask, "What about the heathen man in the jungle who wants to be saved but has never heard the Gospel?" Every sinner must be saved in order to go to Heaven, and God can work miracles to reach seekers with the Gospel.

On the next day, our gracious God taught Peter a powerful lesson about bigotry and the cleansing power of God. This vision was necessary to override Peter's prejudice against the Gentiles so that he would go and preach to them.

**Acts 10:9–23**
*On the morrow, as they went on their journey, and drew nigh unto the city, Peter went up upon the housetop to pray about the sixth hour: And he became very hungry, and would have eaten: but while they made ready, he fell into a trance, And saw heaven opened, and a certain vessel descending unto him, as it had been a great sheet knit at the four corners, and let down to the earth: Wherein were all manner of fourfooted beasts of the earth, and wild beasts, and creeping things, and fowls of the air. And there came a voice to him, Rise, Peter; kill, and eat. But Peter said, Not so, Lord; for I have never eaten any thing that is common or unclean. And the voice spake unto him again the second time, What God hath cleansed, that call not thou common. This was done thrice: and the vessel was received up again into heaven. Now while Peter doubted in himself what this vision which he had seen should mean, behold, the men which were sent from Cornelius had made enquiry for Simon's house, and stood before the gate, And called, and asked whether Simon, which was surnamed Peter, were lodged there. While Peter thought on the vision, the Spirit said unto him, Behold, three men seek thee. Arise*

*therefore, and get thee down, and go with them, doubting nothing: for I have sent them. Then Peter went down to the men which were sent unto him from Cornelius; and said, Behold, I am he whom ye seek: what is the cause wherefore ye are come? And they said, Cornelius the centurion, a just man, and one that feareth God, and of good report among all the nation of the Jews, was warned from God by an holy angel to send for thee into his house, and to hear words of thee. Then called he them in, and lodged them. And on the morrow Peter went away with them, and certain brethren from Joppa accompanied him.*

When Peter arrived at the house of Cornelius, he was greeted with humble adoration. Peter explained that worship was reserved for God alone. To Peter's surprise, the house was full of people waiting to hear him preach! Cornelius had gathered his family and friends to hear the Gospel.

**Acts 10:24–28**
*And the morrow after they entered into Caesarea. And Cornelius waited for them, and had called together his kinsmen and near friends. And as Peter was coming in, Cornelius met him, and fell down at his feet, and worshipped him. But Peter took him up, saying, Stand up; I myself also am a man. And as he talked with him, he went in, and found many that were come together. And he said unto them, Ye know how that it is an unlawful thing for a man that is a Jew to keep company, or come unto one of another nation; but God hath shewed me that I should not call any man common or unclean.*

Peter told the crowd about how God taught him not to call any man common or unclean. Many people today still need to learn this lesson. God loves everyone. The ground is level at the Cross. Cornelius told Peter about the visit from the angel and why he sent for him. Cornelius gathered all these people to hear the Word of God. Peter opened his mouth and preached the glorious Gospel of Christ.

**Acts 10:29–43**
*Therefore came I unto you without gainsaying, as soon as I was sent for: I ask therefore for what intent ye have sent for me? And Cornelius*

# THE BEAUTY OF REMISSION

*said, Four days ago I was fasting until this hour; and at the ninth hour I prayed in my house, and, behold, a man stood before me in bright clothing, And said, Cornelius, thy prayer is heard, and thine alms are had in remembrance in the sight of God. Send therefore to Joppa, and call hither Simon, whose surname is Peter; he is lodged in the house of one Simon a tanner by the sea side: who, when he cometh, shall speak unto thee. Immediately therefore I sent to thee; and thou hast well done that thou art come. Now therefore are we all here present before God, to hear all things that are commanded thee of God. Then Peter opened his mouth, and said, Of a truth I perceive that God is no respecter of persons: But in every nation he that feareth him, and worketh righteousness, is accepted with him. The word which God sent unto the children of Israel, preaching peace by Jesus Christ: (he is Lord of all:) That word, I say, ye know, which was published throughout all Judaea, and began from Galilee, after the baptism which John preached; How God anointed Jesus of Nazareth with the Holy Ghost and with power: who went about doing good, and healing all that were oppressed of the devil; for God was with him. And we are witnesses of all things which he did both in the land of the Jews, and in Jerusalem; whom they slew and hanged on a tree: Him God raised up the third day, and shewed him openly; Not to all the people, but unto witnesses chosen before of God, even to us, who did eat and drink with him after he rose from the dead. And he commanded us to preach unto the people, and to testify that it is he which was ordained of God to be the Judge of quick and dead. To him give all the prophets witness, that through his name whosoever believeth in him shall receive remission of sins.*

What a sermon! Peter ended the sermon with the great truth that *...through his name whosoever believeth in him shall receive remission of sins.* The Holy Ghost fell upon these Gentiles in a visible and audible way to prove that Gentiles could be saved. This event changed the entire focus of the church, revealing that God would save Jews and Gentiles by the same Gospel through the same faith. All who believe in Jesus Christ will receive the remission of sins.

The word *remission* is a synonym for forgiveness. Let us investigate the deeper meaning of this word to further reveal the beauty of our so great salvation. What is the meaning of the word *remission*? Let us consult our trusty Webster's 1828 *American Dictionary of the English Language* to learn the definition of remission.

Remission
REMIS'SION, *n.* [Fr. from L. *remissio,* from *remitto,* to send back.]
1. Abatement; relaxation; moderation; as the *remission* of extreme rigor.    *Bacon.*
2. Abatement; diminution of intensity; as the *remission* of the sun's heat; the *remission* of cold; the *remission* of close study or of labor.    *Woodward. Locke.*
3. Release; discharge or relinquishment of a claim or right; as the *remission* of a tax or duty.    *Addison.*
4. In *medicine,* abatement; a temporary subsidence of the force or violence of a disease or of pain, as distinguished from *intermission,* in which the disease leaves the patient entirely for a time.
5. Forgiveness; pardon; that is, the giving up of the punishment due to a crime; as the *remission* of sins. Matt. xxvi. Heb. ix.
6. The act of sending back. [*Not in use.*]

The word *remission* comes from the verb *remit*. What does the word *remit* mean in the Webster's 1828 Dictionary?

Remit
REMIT', *v. t.* [L. *remitto,* to send back; *re* and *mitto,* to send; Fr. *remettre;* It. *rimettere;* Sp. *remitir.*]
1. To relax, as intensity; to make less tense or violent.
    So willingly doth God *remit* his ire.    *Milton.*
2. To forgive; to surrender the right of punishing a crime; as, to *remit* punishment.    *Dryden.*
3. To pardon, as a fault or crime.
    Whose soever sins ye *remit,* they are *remitted* to them. John xx.
4. To give up; to resign.

> In grievous and inhuman crimes, offenders should be *remitted* to their prince. *Hayward.*

5. To refer; as a clause that *remitted* all to the bishop's discretion. *Bacon.*
6. To send back.
   > The pris'ner was *remitted* to the guard. *Dryden.*
7. To transmit money, bills or other thing in payment for goods received. American merchants *remit* money, bills of exchange or some species of stock, in payment for British goods.
8. To restore.
   > In this case, the law *remits* him to his ancient and more certain right. *Blackstone.*

Now that we know the general definition of the word, let us apply it to Scripture. What does the word *remission* mean in the Bible? Remission highlights the release of the penalty of sin through forgiveness. It is the surrender of the right to punish for a crime. It is the pardon of sin by the release of guilt. **Remission of sins means to release from the guilt and penalty of sins. God removes our sins from us along with the guilt and penaltie s they bring.**

**Psalm 103:12**
*As far as the east is from the west, so far hath he removed our transgressions from us.*

**Micah 7:19**
*He will turn again, he will have compassion upon us; he will subdue our iniquities; and thou wilt cast all their sins into the depths of the sea.*

The Bible explains three great truths about the remission of sins.

### 1. Remission of Sins through Faith in Christ

**Acts 10:43**
*To him give all the prophets witness, that through his name whosoever believeth in him shall receive remission of sins.*

Jesus Christ of Nazareth was the Messiah foretold by thousands of years of prophets. He fulfilled every prophecy of the Old Testament. Through these prophecies, all the prophets gave witness that Jesus is the Christ indeed. Also, the prophets witnessed that through His name, all who believe will receive remission of sins. No more sacrifices were needed. No more holy days or feasts were required. All of these foreshadowed the coming of the Saviour. Now that the Son is risen, we have no need of shadows or types. Remission of sins is by faith alone, by grace alone, and through Christ alone.

## 2. Remission of Sins through Repentance

John used baptism as a proof of repentance that would lead to faith in the coming Messiah.

**Mark 1:4**
*John did baptize in the wilderness, and preach the baptism of repentance for the remission of sins.*

Repentance is a change of mind that leads to a change of actions. Repentance unto salvation is a change of mind about sinfulness and the Saviour that leads one to believe the Gospel.

**Luke 3:3-4**
*And he came into all the country about Jordan, preaching the baptism of repentance for the remission of sins; As it is written in the book of the words of Esaias the prophet, saying, The voice of one crying in the wilderness, Prepare ye the way of the Lord, make his paths straight.*

Zacharias, the father of John the Baptist, prophesied that his son would be the forerunner of the Messiah and would preach the remission of sins.

**Luke 1:77**
*To give knowledge of salvation unto his people by the remission of their sins,*

# THE BEAUTY OF REMISSION

The Great Commission is recorded in all four Gospels and in the book of Acts. When Christ gave the Great Commission to His disciples in the Gospel of Luke, He commanded that repentance and remission of sins be preached among all nations, beginning at home.

**Luke 24:47**
*And that repentance and remission of sins should be preached in his name among all nations, beginning at Jerusalem.*

The word *repent* can be used to signify the entire Gospel including the acknowledgement of sins, the recognition of the Saviour, and personal faith in Christ.

**Acts 2:38**
*Then Peter said unto them, Repent, and be baptized every one of you in the name of Jesus Christ for the remission of sins, and ye shall receive the gift of the Holy Ghost.*

In this passage, Peter exhorted people to repent and then be baptized, pointing to the remission of sins. The word *for* means "pointing to." The phrase *for the remission of sins* means baptism "points to" or indicates the remission of sins. Water baptism cannot wash away sin. Peter never preached that baptism saves. In fact, he preached the opposite.

**I Peter 3:21**
*The like figure whereunto even baptism doth also now save us (not the putting away of the filth of the flesh, but the answer of a good conscience toward God,) by the resurrection of Jesus Christ:*

Baptism does not wash away the sins of the flesh. It saves our consciences from guilt and shame.

### 3. Remission of Sins through Christ's Shed Blood.

**Matthew 26:28**
*For this is my blood of the new testament, which is shed for many for the remission of sins.*

During the Last Supper, our Lord instituted the Lord's Supper to be observed by the New Testament churches. Christ explained that His shed blood is the basis for the new covenant and was offered for the remission of sins.

**Hebrews 9:22**
*And almost all things are by the law purged with blood; and without shedding of blood is no remission.*

The Bible tells us that there is no remission of sins without the shedding of blood. A blood offering is required to satisfy God's justice so that He will forgive our sins.

**Ephesians 1:7**
*In whom we have redemption through his blood, the forgiveness of sins, according to the riches of his grace;*

**Colossians 1:20**
*And, having made peace through the blood of his cross, by him to reconcile all things unto himself; by him, I say, whether they be things in earth, or things in heaven.*

The perfect blood of Jesus Christ was sufficient to pay for the sins of every person who would ever live. The Greek word for *remission* in Romans 3:25 is a different word than is used in the other references to remission in the New Testament.

**Romans 3:23–25**
*For all have sinned, and come short of the glory of God; Being justified freely by his grace through the redemption that is in Christ Jesus: Whom God hath set forth to be a propitiation through faith in his blood, to*

# THE BEAUTY OF REMISSION

*declare his righteousness for the remission of sins that are past, through the forbearance of God;*

The word for *remission* here means "toleration." This verse teaches us that the covering (propitiation) of the blood of Christ allowed God to tolerate the sins of the world without total judgment before the sacrifice of Christ was completed. God was able to forebear the sins of the world until the saving work of Jesus Christ was completed.

**Hebrews 10:16-22**
*This is the covenant that I will make with them after those days, saith the Lord, I will put my laws into their hearts, and in their minds will I write them; And their sins and iniquities will I remember no more. Now where remission of these is, there is no more offering for sin. Having therefore, brethren, boldness to enter into the holiest by the blood of Jesus, By a new and living way, which he hath consecrated for us, through the veil, that is to say, his flesh; And having an high priest over the house of God; Let us draw near with a true heart in full assurance of faith, having our hearts sprinkled from an evil conscience, and our bodies washed with pure water.*

The blood of Jesus Christ cleanses all sin. There is no other offering for sin. Nothing else can cleanse sin, and no other sacrifice is needed after the blood is applied.

Remission of sins means to release from the guilt and penalty of sins. God removes our sins from us along with the guilt and penalties they bring. Through faith in the finished work of Christ, our sins are forgiven. This means we are pardoned from our sins and our guilt. Have your sins been remitted? Are you born again? If not, trust Jesus Christ as your Saviour today! If you have been saved by believing the Gospel, rejoice that your iniquities are forgiven and that your sins are removed from your record. Your sins have been remitted, and you are free in Christ!

## Chapter Eight

# The Beauty of Imputation

Do you know the Bible doctrine of imputation? You should! It is vital to eternal salvation and is illustrative of the surety of Christ's redemption. Discover the power and beauty of this crucial Bible doctrine. Imputation is a benefit of our so great salvation. Without this doctrine, we could not be saved. The doctrine of imputation illustrates the depth and beauty of Christ's redemption.

**Romans 4:1-8**
*What shall we say then that Abraham our father, as pertaining to the flesh, hath found? For if Abraham were justified by works, he hath whereof to glory; but not before God. For what saith the scripture? Abraham believed God, and it was counted unto him for righteousness. Now to him that worketh is the reward not reckoned of grace, but of debt. But to him that worketh not, but believeth on him that justifieth the ungodly, his faith is counted for righteousness. Even as David also describeth the blessedness of the man, unto whom God imputeth righteousness without works, Saying, Blessed are they whose iniquities are forgiven, and whose sins are covered. Blessed is the man to whom the Lord will not impute sin.*

The word *imputation* is an old English word that means "to attribute or ascribe." It means to credit something not possessed to a person's account. The word *impute* is a legal term that means "to ascribe to one person the qualities of another." For example, in some cultures, when a parent dies owing a financial debt, the money owed is imputed to the accounts of the children. The debt becomes theirs even though they did not earn it. This is imputation of debt. In a Scriptural context, Christ's righteousness, through His finished work, is placed on the accounts of sinners. This is imputed righteousness.

Imputation has nothing to do with guilt or innocence. An innocent man can be reckoned as guilty, and a guilty man can be assigned righteousness. Imputation is a legal act of reckoning. Furthermore, imputation does not change character but changes legal standing.

The noun form (imputation) is not found in the King James Bible, but the verb form "impute" is found multiple times and the doctrine is observed often. There are three main concepts of imputation in Scripture.

**1. Imputed Sin**

**Romans 4:8**
*Blessed is the man to whom the Lord will not impute sin.*

It is a blessing when God does not impute sin to our accounts. Yet, the fact remains that sin can be imputed or reckoned to our accounts. The most striking example of imputed sin is found in the beginning of recorded human history. Sin entered the world through the first man, Adam. When Adam chose to sin, his sin passed on to all men.

**Romans 5:12**
*Wherefore, as by one man sin entered into the world, and death by sin; and so death passed upon all men, for that all have sinned:*

When the first man, Adam, sinned, all of our future decisions and DNA were bound up in him. His sin and guilt were imputed to all mankind. We are sinners by birth and by choice. We are born with a sin nature and choose to sin. If we had been in the garden instead of Adam, we would have made the same choice. We are guilty before God.

# THE BEAUTY OF IMPUTATION

**Romans 3:19**
*Now we know that what things soever the law saith, it saith to them who are under the law: that every mouth may be stopped, and all the world may become guilty before God.*

Every sinful soul requires judgment.

**Romans 6:23**
*For the wages of sin is death; but the gift of God is eternal life through Jesus Christ our Lord.*

The dreadful and eternal wrath of God abides upon sinners who have not been forgiven.

**John 3:36**
*He that believeth on the Son hath everlasting life: and he that believeth not the Son shall not see life; but the wrath of God abideth on him.*

The Bible makes a distinction between Adam's sin that was imputed to humanity and the penalty for individuals who sin today. A transgressor will be punished, but that individual's sin is not imputed to innocent children, family, or friends.

**Ezekiel 18:20**
*The soul that sinneth, it shall die. The son shall not bear the iniquity of the father, neither shall the father bear the iniquity of the son: the righteousness of the righteous shall be upon him, and the wickedness of the wicked shall be upon him.*

One person should not be punished for the sins of another.

**I Samuel 22:15**
*Did I then begin to enquire of God for him? be it far from me: let not the king impute any thing unto his servant, nor to all the house of my father: for thy servant knew nothing of all this, less or more.*

Wicked people and governments have used the idea of imputed guilt as a tactic for control and subjugation. Tyrants, Nazis, Communists, etc., have punished or murdered using imputed guilt as a reason.

Today, this dangerous idea is used by socialists and anarchists to cause unrest in America. You are white? Then you are guilty because some white people were guilty. You are American? Then you must be bad because America is terrible and is irredeemable since previous generations of Americans made some bad decisions. Imputation of guilt is a perilous idea which causes classes of people to be punished on social whims.

It is a dangerous game to start imputing the sin and guilt of one person to others. Who made you judge and jury? There is one God. He is the Judge. We all will give an account to Him.

### Hebrews 12:23
*To the general assembly and church of the firstborn, which are written in heaven, and to God the Judge of all, and to the spirits of just men made perfect,*

### 2. Imputed Sacrifice

Christ died on the Cross in the place of sinners. He died to pay for our sins.

### Romans 5:6
*For when we were yet without strength, in due time Christ died for the ungodly.*

### Romans 5:8
*But God commendeth his love toward us, in that, while we were yet sinners, Christ died for us.*

Through faith, our accounts reflect Christ's sacrifice. In the records of God, believers died with Christ and rose again with Him unto salvation.

# THE BEAUTY OF IMPUTATION

**Romans 6:3-11**
*Know ye not, that so many of us as were baptized into Jesus Christ were baptized into his death? Therefore we are buried with him by baptism into death: that like as Christ was raised up from the dead by the glory of the Father, even so we also should walk in newness of life. For if we have been planted together in the likeness of his death, we shall be also in the likeness of his resurrection: Knowing this, that our old man is crucified with him, that the body of sin might be destroyed, that henceforth we should not serve sin. For he that is dead is freed from sin. Now if we be dead with Christ, we believe that we shall also live with him: Knowing that Christ being raised from the dead dieth no more; death hath no more dominion over him. For in that he died, he died unto sin once: but in that he liveth, he liveth unto God. Likewise reckon ye also yourselves to be dead indeed unto sin, but alive unto God through Jesus Christ our Lord.*

Imputed sacrifice was symbolized in the Old Testament system of sacrifices. On the Day of Atonement, the sins of the people were symbolically placed on the head of a goat and it was sent away into the wilderness.

**Leviticus 16:20-22**
*And when he hath made an end of reconciling the holy place, and the tabernacle of the congregation, and the altar, he shall bring the live goat: And Aaron shall lay both his hands upon the head of the live goat, and confess over him all the iniquities of the children of Israel, and all their transgressions in all their sins, putting them upon the head of the goat, and shall send him away by the hand of a fit man into the wilderness: And the goat shall bear upon him all their iniquities unto a land not inhabited: and he shall let go the goat in the wilderness.*

When Christ died on the Cross, all of the sins of all the world were placed upon Him. When you accept Christ as your personal Saviour, His substitutionary death is placed on your account in Heaven.

**I Peter 2:24**
*Who his own self bare our sins in his own body on the tree, that we, being dead to sins, should live unto righteousness: by whose stripes ye were healed.*

Isaiah 53 is filled with substitutionary imagery.

**Isaiah 53:4–11**
*Surely he hath borne our griefs, and carried our sorrows: yet we did esteem him stricken, smitten of God, and afflicted. But he was wounded for our transgressions, he was bruised for our iniquities: the chastisement of our peace was upon him; and with his stripes we are healed. All we like sheep have gone astray; we have turned every one to his own way; and the LORD hath laid on him the iniquity of us all. He was oppressed, and he was afflicted, yet he opened not his mouth: he is brought as a lamb to the slaughter, and as a sheep before her shearers is dumb, so he openeth not his mouth. He was taken from prison and from judgment: and who shall declare his generation? for he was cut off out of the land of the living: for the transgression of my people was he stricken. And he made his grave with the wicked, and with the rich in his death; because he had done no violence, neither was any deceit in his mouth. Yet it pleased the LORD to bruise him; he hath put him to grief: when thou shalt make his soul an offering for sin, he shall see his seed, he shall prolong his days, and the pleasure of the LORD shall prosper in his hand. He shall see of the travail of his soul, and shall be satisfied: by his knowledge shall my righteous servant justify many; for he shall bear their iniquities.*

We should never stop praising our Saviour for taking our punishment and dying in our place. We will praise His name for ever for His eternal love and excellent greatness!

### 3. Imputed Righteousness

Imputed righteousness is God's righteousness applied to our accounts without works. It is a legal reference to our sins being replaced with Christ's righteousness in the records of God.

# THE BEAUTY OF IMPUTATION

**Romans 4:1-5**
*What shall we say then that Abraham our father, as pertaining to the flesh, hath found? For if Abraham were justified by works, he hath whereof to glory; but not before God. For what saith the scripture? Abraham believed God, and it was counted unto him for righteousness. Now to him that worketh is the reward not reckoned of grace, but of debt. But to him that worketh not, but believeth on him that justifieth the ungodly, his faith is counted for righteousness.*

Abraham was counted righteous for his faith, not for his works. Notice the word *counted* in verses 3 and 5 and the word *reckoned* in verse 4. The Greek word used for these words is the same word used for *impute* in verses 6 and 8. These are accounting and legal terms. There is a glaring lack of fuzzy feelings in this passage. Imputation is a calculation of facts and figures rather than a touching love story. The Gospel is the greatest love story known to man, but the love element of our salvation is told through the other beautiful doctrines of salvation we have learned. Imputation is clinical and exact. It calculates our ending balance in God's register of sin and righteousness. The results of imputation are wonderful!

**Romans 4:6-8**
*Even as David also describeth the blessedness of the man, unto whom God imputeth righteousness without works, Saying, Blessed are they whose iniquities are forgiven, and whose sins are covered. Blessed is the man to whom the Lord will not impute sin.*

This passage refers to Psalm 32:1-2.

**Psalm 32:1-2**
*Blessed is he whose transgression is forgiven, whose sin is covered. Blessed is the man unto whom the LORD imputeth not iniquity, and in whose spirit there is no guile.*

Surely, there is no greater blessedness than to stand righteous in the sight of God apart from our own works. Through the vicarious sacrifice of Christ, our iniquities are forgiven and our sins are covered!

**Romans 4:8**
*Blessed is the man to whom the Lord will not impute sin.*

Thanks to the glorious Gospel of Christ, sin is not imputed to us and Christ's righteousness is imputed to our accounts. The doctrine of imputation is clearly revealed in II Corinthians 5:20-21.

**II Corinthians 5:20–21**
*Now then we are ambassadors for Christ, as though God did beseech you by us: we pray you in Christ's stead, be ye reconciled to God. For he hath made him to be sin for us, who knew no sin; that we might be made the righteousness of God in him.*

Imputation speaks of the accounting of salvation. Imagine two ledgers or checkbooks. One ledger itemizes your sin. Every transgression, trespass, and iniquity in your life has been recorded. Another ledger itemizes the righteousness of Christ. During the process of imputation, God Almighty transfers your sin to the ledger of Christ and Christ's righteousness to your ledger. When God looks at you as a believer today, He sees the righteousness of His only begotten Son, Jesus Christ. It is just as if you had never sinned at all! The doctrine of imputation details the nature of the accounting of sins and righteousness.

**Imputation is beautifully described in the book of Philemon.**

The book of Philemon is a letter written from the Apostle Paul to Philemon, who was a great Christian in Colosse. Colosse was a city where Paul started a church, and it was to this church that he wrote the book of Colossians. While in Colosse, Paul had become a close friend of Philemon. He started a church in Philemon's house (verse

2). Paul was such a dear friend of Philemon that he prayed for him constantly (verse 4) and had great confidence in his work (verse 7).

While in prison at Rome, Paul conducted services and witnessed to the prisoners and keepers. One of his converts was a man named Onesimus (verse 10). Onesimus had been Philemon's slave in Colosse. He had taken some of Philemon's money and had run off to Rome (verse 11). Upon arriving in Rome, he was apprehended and placed in prison. There he met the Apostle Paul, was converted under his ministry, and had a desire to go back to Colosse to be with his master, Philemon, again. Paul volunteered to write a letter to Philemon and instructed Onesimus, upon his discharge from prison, to take the letter to Philemon to ask for forgiveness. This small but powerful book of the New Testament is a letter written from Paul to Philemon on behalf of Onesimus.

**Philemon 18**
*If he hath wronged thee, or oweth thee ought, put that on mine account;*

Ponder the spiritual symbolism in this small book.
- Philemon represents God the Father, the wealthy landowner.
- Onesimus, the slave, represents man.
- The taking of the money represents the sin committed by man in the Garden of Eden.
- The running to Rome represents the fall of man and his being separated from God.
- Paul represents Jesus Christ.
- Onesimus meeting Paul in jail represents conversion.
- Paul's interceding to Philemon on behalf of the slave represents Jesus, our Intercessor.
- Paul's request that Philemon receive Onesimus back is a picture of salvation. We can come back to God only through Jesus Christ.
- Paul's request that Onesimus not be received as a slave but as a brother beloved is a picture of our standing in Jesus Christ.
- Paul's request that Onesimus be received as if it were Paul himself coming instead of Onesimus is a beautiful picture that

we shall be like Jesus. We are heirs of God and joint-heirs with Jesus Christ.
- The letter that Paul wrote is a picture of the Word of God.
- The only hope that Onesimus had was that Philemon would honor the word and request of Paul.
- Our only hope for salvation is in the written Word of God. God receives us on the basis of His Word because Jesus is pleading our case.

What a beautiful illustration! Thank God for salvation! Praise the Lord for the beautiful doctrine of imputation.

The doctrine of imputation is a vital element of eternal salvation. Imputation for salvation is the removal of sins from our accounts and the attribution of the righteousness of Christ to our Heavenly records. When God looks at believers, He sees the perfect righteousness of His only begotten Son, Jesus Christ. There are no mistakes in God's records. Through faith in the finished work of Christ, we are clean in His sight—that, my Friend, is beautiful!

## Chapter Nine

# The Beauty of Propitiation

The Bible doctrine of propitiation is a tremendous reminder of God's love and goodness through salvation. Propitiation is a unique word. This old English word is used three times in the King James Bible. What is propitiation? Let us refer to these helpful resources.

*Baker Encyclopedia of the Bible*
Propitiation

> "Propitiation. Turning away of anger by the offering of a gift. The word was often used by the pagans in antiquity, for they thought of their gods as unpredictable beings, liable to become angry with their worshipers for any trifle. When disaster struck it was often thought that a god was angry and was therefore punishing his worshipers. The remedy was to offer a sacrifice without delay. A well-chosen offering would appease the god and put him in a good mood again. This process was called propitiation."

Of course, the Biblical doctrine of propitiation is much deeper than this pagan understanding, but it gives some context. Consider this definition from Webster's 1828 *American Dictionary of the English Language*.

Propitiation
PROPITIATION, *n.* propisia'shon. [Fr.; from *propitiate.*]
  1. The act of appeasing wrath and conciliating the favor of an offended person; the act of making propitious.

2. In *theology*, the atonement or atoning sacrifice offered to God to assuage his wrath and render him propitious to sinners. Christ is the *propitiation* for the sins of men. Rom. iii. I John ii.

Consider these definitions surrounding the word as well.

Propitiatory
PROPI'TIATORY, *adjective.* Having the power to make propitious; as a *propitiatory* sacrifice. *Stillingfleet.*

PROPI''TIATORY, *n.* Among the Jews, the mercy-seat; the lid or cover of the ark of the covenant, lined within and without with plates of gold. This was a type of Christ. *Encyc.*

## The Bible states three times that Jesus Christ is our PROPITIATION.

**Romans 3:25**
*Whom God hath set forth to be a propitiation through faith in his blood, to declare his righteousness for the remission of sins that are past, through the forbearance of God;*

**I John 2:2**
*And he is the propitiation for our sins: and not for ours only, but also for the sins of the whole world.*

**I John 4:10**
*Herein is love, not that we loved God, but that he loved us, and sent his Son to be the propitiation for our sins.*

What does Jesus Christ being our propitiation mean? Consider four truths that demonstrate the beauty of this illustration of salvation.

### 1. Propitiation is a covering.

# THE BEAUTY OF PROPITIATION

God covers our sins. In the Old Testament, God would cover the sins year by year. They were not fully paid for until the Messiah completed the Gospel plan. However, the symbolic sacrifices withheld God's judgment until Christ paid the final price for sin.

**Romans 4:7**
*Saying, Blessed are they whose iniquities are forgiven, and whose sins are covered.*

Because of the sacrifice of Christ, our sins are covered once and for all!

### 2. Propitiation speaks of appeasing wrath.

In many cultures, a gift or an offering would be given to an offended party to pacify wrath. Likewise, the selfless sacrifice of Christ saved us from God's wrath.

**Romans 5:9**
*Much more then, being now justified by his blood, we shall be saved from wrath through him.*

### 3. Propitiation restores favor.

A great gift could not only appease wrath but also obtain favor. Two synonyms of the word *favor* are *grace* and *kindness*. Jesus Christ purchased our salvation and restored God's grace and kindness to those who believe upon Him.

**Ephesians 2:7**
*That in the ages to come he might shew the exceeding riches of his grace in his kindness toward us through Christ Jesus.*

### 4. Among the Jews, propitiation spoke of the mercy seat.

# THE BEAUTY OF SALVATION

The Mercy Seat is the lid, or cover, of the Ark of the Covenant. It was a type of Christ. During the Offering of Atonement, sacrificial blood was spread on the Mercy Seat for recompense of sins.

**Leviticus 16:13–14**
*And he shall put the incense upon the fire before the LORD, that the cloud of the incense may cover the mercy seat that is upon the testimony, that he die not: And he shall take of the blood of the bullock, and sprinkle it with his finger upon the mercy seat eastward; and before the mercy seat shall he sprinkle of the blood with his finger seven times.*

The doctrine of propitiation highlights Jesus Christ as the ultimate covering for sin. There is no more need for the sacrifice of bulls and goats. Christ is our Atonement!

**Hebrews 9:11–15**
*But Christ being come an high priest of good things to come, by a greater and more perfect tabernacle, not made with hands, that is to say, not of this building; Neither by the blood of goats and calves, but by his own blood he entered in once into the holy place, having obtained eternal redemption for us. For if the blood of bulls and of goats, and the ashes of an heifer sprinkling the unclean, sanctifieth to the purifying of the flesh: How much more shall the blood of Christ, who through the eternal Spirit offered himself without spot to God, purge your conscience from dead works to serve the living God? And for this cause he is the mediator of the new testament, that by means of death, for the redemption of the transgressions that were under the first testament, they which are called might receive the promise of eternal inheritance.*

Can you see the beauty of your salvation in the doctrine of propitiation? Jesus Christ was the ultimate Sacrifice. He paid the sufficient price for our sins, appeased God's wrath, and purchased our eternal favor.

## Chapter Ten

# The Beauty of Justification

Justification is a vital doctrine that explains the beauty and fullness of eternal salvation. Have you been justified?

**Romans 5:16-18**
*And not as it was by one that sinned, so is the gift: for the judgment was by one to condemnation, but the free gift is of many offences unto justification. For if by one man's offence death reigned by one; much more they which receive abundance of grace and of the gift of righteousness shall reign in life by one, Jesus Christ.) Therefore as by the offence of one judgment came upon all men to condemnation; even so by the righteousness of one the free gift came upon all men unto justification of life.*

The *word justify* is used regularly in conversation today. You can justify:
- Your words in a document
- Your actions
- Someone else's actions

The word *justify* has many definitions. It means "to prove or show to be just or righteous, to defend, to clear from guilt; to prove or show innocent

What is justification? Let us consult our Webster's 1828 *American Dictionary of the English Language*.

Justification
JUSTIFIϾA'TION, *n.* [Fr. from *justifier,* to *justify.*]
1. The act of justifying; a showing to be just or conformable to law, rectitude or propriety; vindication; defense. The court listened to the evidence and arguments in *justification* of the prisoner's conduct. Our disobedience to God's commands admits no *justification.*
2. Absolution.
   > I hope, for my brother's *justification,* he wrote this but as an essay of my virtue. — *Shak.*
3. In *law,* the showing of a sufficient reason in court why a defendant did what he is called to answer. Pleas in *justification* must set forth some special matter.
4. In *theology,* remission of sin and absolution from guilt and punishment; or an act of free grace by which God pardons the sinner and accepts him as righteous, on account of the atonement of Christ.

Read this instructive excerpt from the *Baker Encyclopedia of the Bible.*

Justification

Justification. The act of God in bringing sinners into a new covenant relationship with himself through the forgiveness of sins. Along with such terms as "regeneration" and "reconciliation," it relates to a basic aspect of conversion. It is a declarative act of God by which he establishes persons as righteous; that is, in right and true relationship to himself.

Since the time of the Reformation, when Martin Luther reestablished the doctrine of justification by faith alone as the cornerstone for theological understanding, this term has had special significance in the history of theology. To Luther it represented a rediscovery of Paul and a fundamental counterthrust to medieval Catholicism with its theology of works and indulgences. The doctrine of justification by faith alone affirms the thoroughgoing sinfulness of all persons, their total inability to deal effectively with their own sin, and the gracious provision through the death of Jesus Christ of a complete atonement for sin, to which persons respond in simple trust without any special claims or merit of their own.

When it comes to salvation, the doctrine of justification is very specific. It is a legal term that means "to declare righteous." Through faith in Christ, God imputes the perfect righteousness of Christ to our accounts, as we learned in the last chapter. Justification is God's legal pronouncement that we are cleansed from sin. A good way to remember this doctrine is that JUSTIFICTION means God looks at saved individuals as if they never sinned. Those who have been justified can say it is "just as if I never sinned." Our records have been expunged! We have been fully pardoned! There is no guilt or shame in the sight of God! There is no indication that we were ever sinners in the first place. Hallelujah! The blood of Christ cleanses us from EVERY SIN!

I love the following verses. They compare who we used to be before salvation with our condition after we are born again.

**I Corinthians 6:9–11**
*Know ye not that the unrighteous shall not inherit the kingdom of God? Be not deceived: neither fornicators, nor idolaters, nor adulterers, nor effeminate, nor abusers of themselves with mankind, Nor thieves, nor covetous, nor drunkards, nor revilers, nor extortioners, shall inherit the kingdom of God. And such were some of you: but ye are washed, but ye are sanctified, but ye are justified in the name of the Lord Jesus, and by the Spirit of our God.*

Such were some of you! I may not be everything I ought to be, but praise God I am not who I used to be! I have been washed, sanctified, and justified in the eyes of God through Christ Jesus.

Notice the revelation of the doctrine of justification in the Bible.

### 1. Justification was PROMISED in the Old Testament.

**Isaiah 45:25**
*In the LORD shall all the seed of Israel be justified, and shall glory.*

**Isaiah 53:11**
*He shall see of the travail of his soul, and shall be satisfied: by his knowledge shall my righteous servant justify many; for he shall bear their iniquities.*

The Gospel was foreshadowed in the Abrahamic Covenant in Genesis 12.

**Galatians 3:8**
*And the scripture, foreseeing that God would justify the heathen through faith, preached before the gospel unto Abraham, saying, In thee shall all nations be blessed.*

It was always God's plan to justify sinners through faith in Christ.

### 2. Justification was PROHIBITED by man's works.

Mankind could not justify themselves no matter how hard they tried.

**Job 9:2–3**
*I know it is so of a truth: but how should man be just with God? If he will contend with him, he cannot answer him one of a thousand.*

**Job 9:20**
*If I justify myself, mine own mouth shall condemn me: if I say, I am perfect, it shall also prove me perverse.*

We can never be justified and saved by the law that we have broken.

# THE BEAUTY OF JUSTIFICATION

**Acts 13:39**
*And by him all that believe are justified from all things, from which ye could not be justified by the law of Moses.*

**Romans 3:20**
*Therefore by the deeds of the law there shall no flesh be justified in his sight: for by the law is the knowledge of sin.*

The law proves us guilty. Only the guilty need justification. Only the sick need a doctor. Only the lost need a Saviour.

### 3. Justification was PERFORMED by Christ Jesus.

Only the perfect sacrifice of Christ as a sufficient payment for our sins could justify us in God's sight.

**Romans 3:22-24**
*Even the righteousness of God which is by faith of Jesus Christ unto all and upon all them that believe: for there is no difference: For all have sinned, and come short of the glory of God; Being justified freely by his grace through the redemption that is in Christ Jesus:*

The phrase *freely by his grace* speaks of the free love and favor of God offered freely through the Gospel of Christ. Justification is based on redemption. It is not a mere verbal allocation but a legal verdict based on the sufficient sacrifice of Christ.

What if you were accused of a crime? There is a large difference between a loving family member saying you are innocent and a full legal verdict from the judge declaring your innocence. Justification is the Judge of the universe declaring that you are innocent!

**Romans 3:25-26**
*Whom God hath set forth to be a propitiation through faith in his blood, to declare his righteousness for the remission of sins that are past, through the forbearance of God; To declare, I say, at this time his righteousness: that he might be just, and the justifier of him which believeth in Jesus.*

# THE BEAUTY OF SALVATION

Jesus Christ is called the JUST JUSTIFIER. I love it! Jesus did not die for His own sins. He was already JUST before God. He died to justify us. The shed blood of Jesus Christ was the sufficient payment for the sins of the world.

**Romans 5:9**
*Much more then, being now justified by his blood, we shall be saved from wrath through him.*

### 4. Justification is PROCURED by faith in the Gospel.

The word *procure* means "to get or gain; to obtain." Justification can be obtained only through personal faith in the death, burial, and resurrection of Jesus Christ. Justification is by faith without the deeds of the law. You cannot save yourself by good works, religious activity, or good intentions.

**Romans 3:28**
*Therefore we conclude that a man is justified by faith without the deeds of the law.*

Only faith in Jesus Christ can justify sinners.

**Romans 3:30**
*Seeing it is one God, which shall justify the circumcision by faith, and uncircumcision through faith.*

We are not justified by:
- Circumcision
- Baptism
- Good works
- Sacraments
- Indulgences
- Offerings
- Confession
- Religion

# THE BEAUTY OF JUSTIFICATION

We are justified by faith alone, through grace alone, and in Christ alone!

**Romans 5:1**
*Therefore being justified by faith, we have peace with God through our Lord Jesus Christ:*

**Galatians 2:16**
*Knowing that a man is not justified by the works of the law, but by the faith of Jesus Christ, even we have believed in Jesus Christ, that we might be justified by the faith of Christ, and not by the works of the law: for by the works of the law shall no flesh be justified.*

**Galatians 3:24**
*Wherefore the law was our schoolmaster to bring us unto Christ, that we might be justified by faith.*

Those who try to earn salvation by works are not seeking grace. They are rejecting it.

**Galatians 5:4**
*Christ is become of no effect unto you, whosoever of you are justified by the law; ye are fallen from grace.*

The term *fallen from grace* does not mean that we lose our salvation. Rather, it means that we fall short of receiving God's grace because we are seeking to justify ourselves. Through justification, God looks at us as if we have always kept His perfect law. He sees the saved as if they have never sinned.

### 5. Justification is PERFECTED by works.

Good works do not save us. They show the world that we have been saved.

**James 2:22**
*Seest thou how faith wrought with his works, and by works was faith made perfect?*

The words *made perfect* here mean "completed" or "fulfilled." Here is the eternal question:

**James 2:14**
*What doth it profit, my brethren, though a man say he hath faith, and have not works? can faith save him?*

James 2:1-13 teaches Christians not to live by what we SEE but by what we know God's Word SAYS. Verses 14-26 tell us the unbelievers live by what they SEE and not by what we SAY. THIS PASSAGE IS NOT A DISCUSSION OF THE NECESSITY OF WORKS FOR SALVATION. We have proven already from the Bible that works have no part in our redemption. Christ alone can save us from our sins. This portion of Scripture demonstrates the difference between what we SAY and what others SEE. You cannot see the salvation in my heart. You can see my actions.

**We are JUSTIFIED IN THE SIGHT OF GOD by our faith. We are JUSTIFIED IN THE SIGHT OF MAN by our works.**

That is why hypocrisy is such a terrible sin. It betrays the work of God in our hearts. Sin in the lives of believers gives the enemies of the Lord an opportunity to blaspheme and continue in stubborn unbelief. James 2:14 reminds us that our declaration of faith is unprofitable to the rest of the world if we do not have the works to back up our professions.

Do you strive to live like Christ? Your daily life choices may mean the difference between Heaven or Hell to the world around you. God receives the glory when we walk worthy of our Christian title. Satan wins the victory when we tarnish the name of Christ by a wavering profession. WE HAVE BEEN JUSTIFIED! LIVE LIKE IT!

# THE BEAUTY OF JUSTIFICATION

I love the chorus of the song "Justified."
I'm justified! I'm happy in Jesus today.
The sins I've committed, they're all in the past;
They've all been forgiven, and He holds me fast!
I'm justified! I'm justified!
I'm happy in Jesus today!

Have you been JUSTIFIED? Will you trust Jesus Christ as your Saviour today? If you have been justified, God looks at you as if you have never sinned. Strive to live up to His so great salvation. Take a moment to thank God for His beautiful salvation!

## Chapter Eleven

# The Beauty of Sanctification

What is sanctification? What are the two types of sanctification? How is God working to sanctify you today? Find out the answers to these questions as well as how God's sanctifying work saves your soul and improves your life.

**I Corinthians 1:1-2**
*Paul, called to be an apostle of Jesus Christ through the will of God, and Sosthenes our brother, Unto the church of God which is at Corinth, to them that are sanctified in Christ Jesus, called to be saints, with all that in every place call upon the name of Jesus Christ our Lord, both theirs and ours:*

Sanctification is a foundational Bible doctrine. The concept is found throughout the Bible. A faithful Bible preacher will invoke the doctrine of sanctification regularly. Sanctification begins at salvation and continues in your life today. God is using it to help you become the person you were created to be.

Sanctification is a big word that is not used in daily communication. It is important that we have the correct definition to understand the vital doctrine. What is sanctification? Generally, sanctification means "to be made holy or purified and set apart for God." It has a broad use in Scripture. Synonyms are consecrated, sacred, holy, hallowed, and dedicated. Once again, let us consult Webster's 1828 *American Dictionary of the English Language* to find out the definition.

## Sanctification

SANCTIFICA'TION, *n.* [Fr. from Low L. *sanctificatio,* from *sanctifico.* See *Sanctify.*]

1. The act of making holy. In an evangelical sense, the act of God's grace by which the affections of men are purified or alienated from sin and the world, and exalted to a supreme love to God.

    God hath from the beginning chosen you to salvation, through *sanctification* of the Spirit and belief of the truth. 2 Thess. ii. 1 Pet. 1.

2. The act of consecrating or of setting apart for a sacred purpose; consecration. *Stilling fleet.*

    The word *sanctification* comes from the word *sanctify.*

## Sanctify

SANC'TIFY, *v. tr.* [Fr. *sanctifier;* It. *santificare;* Sp. *santificar;* Low L. *sanctifico;* from *sanctus,* holy, and *facio,* to make.]

1. In *a general sense,* to cleanse, purify or make holy. *Addison.*
2. To separate, set apart or appoint to a holy, sacred or religious use.

    God blessed the seventh day and *sanctified* it. Gen. ii.

    So under the Jewish dispensation, to *sanctify* the altar, the temple, the priests, &c.

3. To purify; to prepare for divine service, and for partaking of holy things. Ex. xix.
4. To separate, ordain and appoint to the work of redemption and the government of the church. John x.
5. To cleanse from corruption; to purify from sin; to make holy by detaching the affections from the world and its defilements, and exalting them to a supreme love to God.

    *Sanctify* them through thy truth; thy word is truth. John xvii. Eph. 5.

6. To make the means of holiness; to render productive of holiness or piety.

    Those judgments of God are the more welcome, as a means which his mercy hath *sanctified* so to me, as to make me repent of that unjust act. *K. Charles.*

7. To make free from guilt.
   > That holy man, amaz'd at what he saw,
   > Made haste to *sanctify* the bliss by law.  *Dryden.*
8. To secure from violation.
   > Truth guards the poet, *sanctifies* the line.  *Pope.*

*To sanctify* God, to praise and celebrate him as a holy being; to acknowledge and honor his holy majesty, and to reverence his character and laws. Isaiah 8:13.

*God sanctifies himself or his name,* by vindicating his honor from the reproaches of the wicked, and manifesting his glory. Ezek. xxxvi.

With those definitions, we are starting to understand this important doctrine. The word *sanctify* means "to set apart for God." People, places, and things can be sanctified. For example, our church building is sanctified. It is set apart for God. The Old Testament tabernacle and temple were sanctified. They were special places used for the worship of God. The furniture and tools of those places were sacred. They were only used in service to the Almighty. Aaron and his sons were hallowed. They were anointed to be priests. As such, they were separated from the congregation and worked for God.

God's Word is called the Holy Bible. It is a Divine Book written by God for His people. It is separated and is distinct from every other book on Earth. I love this truth. Through salvation, believers are sanctified. We are made holy and are set apart for God. There are two types of sanctification in Scripture regarding salvation.
- Positional Sanctification
- Personal Sanctification

Both doctrines are summed up this way in the New Hampshire Baptist Confession of 1833.

*Baker Encyclopedia of the Bible*
Sanctification

> A comprehensive definition of sanctification by the New Hampshire Baptist Confession (1833) states: "We believe that sanctification is the process by which, according to the

will of God, we are made partakers of his holiness; that it is a progressive work; that it is begun in regeneration; and that it is carried on in the hearts of believers by the presence and power of the Holy Spirit, the Sealer and Comforter, in the continual use of the appointed means—especially the Word of God, self-examination, self-denial, watchfulness, and prayer" (Article X).

Let us investigate God's Word to learn the beauty of the doctrine of sanctification.

### 1. Positional Sanctification

What is positional sanctification? It is also known as imputed salvation. It is a by-product of salvation by which we are cleaned, purified, and set apart for God alone.

#### A. All believers are sanctified.

**I Corinthians 6:11**
*And such were some of you: but ye are washed, but ye are sanctified, but ye are justified in the name of the Lord Jesus, and by the Spirit of our God.*

Three benefits of salvation are mentioned in this verse.
- We are washed – cleansed from our sins by the precious blood of Christ.
- We are sanctified – set apart for God.
- We are justified – our sin records are expunged.

So many miracles happen when a sinner trusts Christ. Praise God for His so great salvation! Once a sinner trusts Christ as Saviour, he is purchased by God. He becomes God's sacred property.

**I Corinthians 6:19–20**
*What? know ye not that your body is the temple of the Holy Ghost which is in you, which ye have of God, and ye are not your own? For ye are*

*bought with a price: therefore glorify God in your body, and in your spirit, which are God's.*

According to these verses, God owns us completely. Our bodies and our spirits belong to God. We have been purified and set apart for God through Christ's saving power. The surrounding verses which give context to this passage explain that we should live holy like God, rejecting the lusts of the flesh and common sins of the culture in which we live.

The Bible declares this truth many times. All born-again Christians are sanctified in Christ Jesus.

**Acts 20:32**
*And now, brethren, I commend you to God, and to the word of his grace, which is able to build you up, and to give you an inheritance among all them which are sanctified.*

Believers are sanctified by faith in Jesus. At the moment of regeneration, we are made the sacred property of God.

**Acts 26:18**
*To open their eyes, and to turn them from darkness to light, and from the power of Satan unto God, that they may receive forgiveness of sins, and inheritance among them which are sanctified by faith that is in me.*

We are entirely (wholly) sanctified by God through Christ Jesus.

**I Thessalonians 5:23**
*And the very God of peace sanctify you wholly; and I pray God your whole spirit and soul and body be preserved blameless unto the coming of our Lord Jesus Christ.*

What a glorious truth! The complete trinity of man (body, soul, and spirit) is sanctified and preserved blameless until we see Christ. The sacrificial death, burial, and resurrection of Jesus Christ sanctifies us in the eyes of God.

**Hebrews 10:10**
*By the which will we are sanctified through the offering of the body of Jesus Christ once for all.*

**Hebrews 13:12**
*Wherefore Jesus also, that he might sanctify the people with his own blood, suffered without the gate.*

Believers become saints and are made holy from the moment of redemption.

**Hebrews 3:1**
*Wherefore, holy brethren, partakers of the heavenly calling, consider the Apostle and High Priest of our profession, Christ Jesus;*

**Philippians 1:1**
*Paul and Timotheus, the servants of Jesus Christ, to all the saints in Christ Jesus which are at Philippi, with the bishops and deacons:*

Each Person of the Godhead (Trinity) is involved in our sanctification.

- **God the Father sanctifies us.**

**Jude 1**
*Jude, the servant of Jesus Christ, and brother of James, to them that are sanctified by God the Father, and preserved in Jesus Christ, and called:*

- **God the Son sanctifies us.**

**Hebrews 13:12**
*Wherefore Jesus also, that he might sanctify the people with his own blood, suffered without the gate.*

- **God the Spirit sanctifies us.**

# THE BEAUTY OF SANCTIFICATION

**Romans 15:16**
*That I should be the minister of Jesus Christ to the Gentiles, ministering the gospel of God, that the offering up of the Gentiles might be acceptable, being sanctified by the Holy Ghost.*

### B. Positional sanctification makes us one with Christ.

**Hebrews 2:11**
*For both he that sanctifieth and they who are sanctified are all of one: for which cause he is not ashamed to call them brethren,*

Christ is sanctified and sanctifies us. We are made the children of God and joint heirs with Christ through the marvelous work of sanctification.

**Romans 8:17**
*And if children, then heirs; heirs of God, and joint-heirs with Christ; if so be that we suffer with him, that we may be also glorified together.*

### C. Positional sanctification sets us apart for service.

**Jeremiah 1:5**
*Before I formed thee in the belly I knew thee; and before thou camest forth out of the womb I sanctified thee, and I ordained thee a prophet unto the nations.*

God has created each one of us for His service. There is a job for you to do in the work of the Almighty. Some are created to be preachers, pastors, missionaries, or evangelists. Others are created to be teachers, helpers, or workers. We all are expected to be soulwinners.

**Ephesians 2:10**
*For we are his workmanship, created in Christ Jesus unto good works, which God hath before ordained that we should walk in them.*

Discover your spiritual gifts and get busy serving the King of kings!

### 2. Personal Sanctification

Positional sanctification sets us apart for God through redemption. We belong to God and have been marked as His own children. This happens immediately at salvation.

**Personal sanctification is the practice of living as if we belong to God.** It is a process rather than an instantaneous action. It is God's will that each believer lives in sanctification by abstaining from sinning.

**I Thessalonians 4:3**
*For this is the will of God, even your sanctification, that ye should abstain from fornication*:

The Holy Spirit accomplishes the work of personal sanctification in us as we surrender to God and are delivered from lust. The Holy Spirit changes us to be like Christ.

**II Corinthians 3:18**
*But we all, with open face beholding as in a glass the glory of the Lord, are changed into the same image from glory to glory, even as by the Spirit of the Lord.*

We are being conformed in the image of God's perfect Son. The Holy Ghost accomplishes this miraculous work.

**Romans 8:29**
*For whom he did foreknow, he also did predestinate to be conformed to the image of his Son, that he might be the firstborn among many brethren.*

# THE BEAUTY OF SANCTIFICATION

The Holy Spirit uses the Word of God to change us from the inside.

**John 17:17-19**
*Sanctify them through thy truth: thy word is truth. As thou hast sent me into the world, even so have I also sent them into the world. And for their sakes I sanctify myself, that they also might be sanctified through the truth.*

Personal sanctification is accomplished faster when we choose to live holy lives. We are commanded to live holy lives and to be separated from sin.

**I Peter 1:15-16**
*But as he which hath called you is holy, so be ye holy in all manner of conversation; Because it is written, Be ye holy; for I am holy.*

**II Corinthians 6:17**
*Wherefore come out from among them, and be ye separate, saith the Lord, and touch not the unclean thing; and I will receive you,*

Christ broke the chains of our bondage to sin through salvation. Christians do not need to sin. We have a choice. Choose to live righteously by saying no to sin.

**Romans 6:11-14**
*Likewise reckon ye also yourselves to be dead indeed unto sin, but alive unto God through Jesus Christ our Lord. Let not sin therefore reign in your mortal body, that ye should obey it in the lusts thereof. Neither yield ye your members as instruments of unrighteousness unto sin: but yield yourselves unto God, as those that are alive from the dead, and your members as instruments of righteousness unto God. For sin shall not have dominion over you: for ye are not under the law, but under grace.*

Our complete sanctification will be accomplished when we see the Lord.

## THE BEAUTY OF SALVATION

**I John 3:2**
*Beloved, now are we the sons of God, and it doth not yet appear what we shall be: but we know that, when he shall appear, we shall be like him; for we shall see him as he is.*

In death, we will leave this corrupt flesh behind, forever separated from sin, and will be glorified eternally with our Lord. What a day that will be!

"What a Day That Will Be"
There is coming a day, when no heart aches shall come,
No more clouds in the sky, no more tears to dim the eye,
All is peace forever more, on that happy golden shore,
What a day, glorious day that will be.

There'll be no sorrow there, no more burdens to bear,
No more sickness, no pain, no more parting over there;
And forever I will be, with the One who died for me,
What a day, glorious day that will be.

CHORUS
What a day that will be, when my Jesus I shall see,
And I look upon His face, the One who saved me by His grace;
When He takes me by the hand, and leads me through the
    Promised Land,
What a day, glorious day that will be.

At the moment of salvation, we are sanctified positionally by being made holy and being set apart for God. We belong to Him. After salvation, we are sanctified practically as the Holy Spirit works to conform us into the likeness of Jesus Christ in our daily lives as we are delivered from the power of sin. Thank God for the beautiful doctrine of sanctification!

## Chapter Twelve

# The Beauty of Glorification

Glorification is the culmination of the doctrines of salvation. It is the completion of all God's promises to His children. Discover the beauty of salvation through the doctrine of glorification.

**Romans 8:29–30**
*For whom he did foreknow, he also did predestinate to be conformed to the image of his Son, that he might be the firstborn among many brethren. Moreover whom he did predestinate, them he also called: and whom he called, them he also justified: and whom he justified, them he also glorified.*

I settled my salvation as a sixteen-year-old boy on a Saturday night after a youth revival. I did not have a terrible life, but I was empty inside. My parents did the best they could to rear me right, but we had our struggles. There were needs in my life that only God could address. I was so thankful to be saved! I still remember laying my head on my pillow to go to sleep on that Saturday night and thinking to myself, "If I die, I am going to Heaven." I think I went to sleep with a smile on my face that night.

As excited as I was to be born again, I had no idea just how incredible salvation was! I have spent a lifetime studying God's Word, and I am continually amazed at the depth, breadth, and height of God's love toward us through salvation.

In this final chapter of *The Beauty of Salvation*, I am excited to address the ultimate outcome of our salvation. Glorification is the summit of salvation. It is the climax of Christendom. It is the fulfillment of our so great salvation. Read our text verses again.

**Romans 8:29–30**
*For whom he did foreknow, he also did predestinate to be conformed to the image of his Son, that he might be the firstborn among many brethren. Moreover whom he did predestinate, them he also called: and whom he called, them he also justified: and whom he justified, them he also glorified.*

The words *whom he did foreknow* in verse 29 refer to *them that love God* in verse 28. In these two delightful verses, God gives us an overview of salvation. They cover the doctrines of:
- Foreknowledge
- Predestination
- Conformation
- Invitation
- Justification
- Glorification

While it would be a worthwhile study, it is not the purpose of this chapter to unpack all of the nuggets of truth in these verses. Allow me to give a brief summary of these verses to lay the foundation so that we may better understand the doctrine of glorification.

God already knows who will get saved. He decided ahead of time that every believer would be conformed to the image of His Son. As a result, God calls all to salvation. Those who accept Christ are made clean in the sight of God. They will inherit God's glory and be brought to their final state of glory. We are told this truth in Romans 8:17-18.

**Romans 8:17–18**
*And if children, then heirs; heirs of God, and joint-heirs with Christ; if so be that we suffer with him, that we may be also glorified together. For I reckon that the sufferings of this present time are not worthy to be compared with the glory which shall be revealed in us.*

These elements unfold in succession and make up one complete salvation. The past tense of the verbs in our text reveals that these actions were decided in the past and are as good as done in the mind of God. The words of the song "At Calvary" draw an enlightening picture.

> O the love that drew salvation's plan!
> O the grace that bro't it down to man!
> O the mighty gulf that God did span
> At Calvary!

In eternity past, the Godhead settled the Gospel plan. It was decided that the Son of God would die for the sins of the world as the perfect God-man. The life of Christ played out exactly as they had predetermined.

**Acts 2:23**
*Him, being delivered by the determinate counsel and foreknowledge of God, ye have taken, and by wicked hands have crucified and slain:*

Since God is eternal and is living outside of linear time, He knows the end from the beginning and the beginning from the end.

**Revelation 21:6**
*And he said unto me, It is done. I am Alpha and Omega, the beginning and the end. I will give unto him that is athirst of the fountain of the water of life freely.*

Notice the past tense in the following verse. Our salvation is so complete that we are already in Heaven with Christ in God's mind!

**Ephesians 2:6**
*And hath raised us up together, and made us sit together in heavenly places in Christ Jesus:*

Now that we have a bit of context from our text verses, let us address the most pressing question of this chapter.

## What is Glorification?

Literally, the word *glory* means "brightness, luster, splendor, or magnificence." The Old Testament word for *glory* means "heavy or weighty." Another definition for the word *glory* is "praise, honor, or adoration." We glorify God with words and actions that give honor, offer praise, or point others to His glory. The word *glorification* is not found in the Bible, but the doctrine is found throughout Scripture. Glorification is the act of giving glory. Let us consult our trusty Webster's 1828 *American Dictionary of the English Language* one more time.

Glorification
GLORIFICA'TION, n. [See *Glorify.*] The act of giving glory or of ascribing honors to. *Taylor.*
2. Exaltation to honor and dignity; elevation to glory; as the *glorification* of Christ after his resurrection.

There are four more facts we need to consider before we continue.

- **God is glorious.**

**Exodus 15:6**
*Thy right hand, O LORD, is become glorious in power: thy right hand, O LORD, hath dashed in pieces the enemy.*

**Exodus 15:11**
*Who is like unto thee, O LORD, among the gods? who is like thee, glorious in holiness, fearful in praises, doing wonders?*

- **We are commanded to glorify God.**

**Psalm 86:12**
*I will praise thee, O Lord my God, with all my heart: and I will glorify thy name for evermore.*

# THE BEAUTY OF GLORIFICATION

**Matthew 5:16**
*Let your light so shine before men, that they may see your good works, and glorify your Father which is in heaven.*

- **Through salvation and glorification, God shares His glory with us.**

**Philippians 3:20–21**
*For our conversation is in heaven; from whence also we look for the Saviour, the Lord Jesus Christ: Who shall change our vile body, that it may be fashioned like unto his glorious body, according to the working whereby he is able even to subdue all things unto himself.*

- **We will inherit eternal glory through saving faith in Jesus Christ.**

**Romans 8:17–18**
*And if children, then heirs; heirs of God, and joint-heirs with Christ; if so be that we suffer with him, that we may be also glorified together. For I reckon that the sufferings of this present time are not worthy to be compared with the glory which shall be revealed in us.*

Wow! To think that God would share His eternal glory with us is humbling. What an unspeakable gift! We will be glorified by God to be with Him in glory forever. It does not get any better than that, my Friend!

As you complete this book by learning about the incredible promise of glorification, allow your heart to swell with praise and adoration for our gracious God. He is amazing!

### 1. The START of Glorification

The process of glorification begins at salvation. The new birth is the beginning of all the eternal good God has planned for His children.

**John 3:3**
*Jesus answered and said unto him, Verily, verily, I say unto thee, Except a man be born again, he cannot see the kingdom of God.*

**II Corinthians 5:17**
*Therefore if any man be in Christ, he is a new creature: old things are passed away; behold, all things are become new.*

When we trust Christ, we are justified. Our accounts with God are settled. When God looks at us, He sees the righteousness of Christ. It is just as if we never sinned at all!

**Romans 3:20–25**
*Therefore by the deeds of the law there shall no flesh be justified in his sight: for by the law is the knowledge of sin. But now the righteousness of God without the law is manifested, being witnessed by the law and the prophets; Even the righteousness of God which is by faith of Jesus Christ unto all and upon all them that believe: for there is no difference: For all have sinned, and come short of the glory of God; Being justified freely by his grace through the redemption that is in Christ Jesus: Whom God hath set forth to be a propitiation through faith in his blood, to declare his righteousness for the remission of sins that are past, through the forbearance of God;*

Have you been justified? When did you trust Christ as your personal Saviour? Justification is the start of the glorification process.

## 2. The SEQUENCE of Glorification

Our text verses show us the order of God's saving work in our lives. Let us look at the linear progression of God's saving work in us. When you were born again, God saved you to the uttermost. You will never be more saved than you were at the moment you trusted Christ. Like a physical birth, the new birth occurs in a specific moment of time. Justification is an event, not a process. Nevertheless, full salvation takes place in three parts:

# THE BEAUTY OF GLORIFICATION

- **Salvation** – Occurs in the **Past** – *We were saved from the **penalty** of sin.*
- **Sanctification** – Happens in the **Present** – *We are saved from the **power** of sin.*
- **Glorification** – Comes in the **Future** – *We will be saved from the **presence** of sin.*

Consider these three concepts to help you understand the fullness of salvation.

## Salvation

**Romans 1:16**
*For I am not ashamed of the gospel of Christ: for it is the power of God unto salvation to every one that believeth; to the Jew first, and also to the Greek.*

**Acts 16:31**
*And they said, Believe on the Lord Jesus Christ, and thou shalt be saved, and thy house.*

Salvation took place the moment you were born again. Many incredible things happened when you put your trust in Jesus Christ as your Saviour. Your sins were forgiven. You were born into the family of God. You were sealed with the Holy Spirit. Your place in Heaven was reserved. Your eternal inheritance was assured. The list of God's goodness toward us through salvation is far too extensive for us to record here.

At salvation, you were saved from the penalty of sin, but your redeemed soul still resides in a fleshly body that has sinful desires. You have two natures battling for control. That is why we face temptation and need sanctification.

## Sanctification

**I Thessalonians 4:4**
*That every one of you should know how to possess his vessel in sanctification and honour;*

**I Thessalonians 5:23**
*And the very God of peace sanctify you wholly; and I pray God your whole spirit and soul and body be preserved blameless unto the coming of our Lord Jesus Christ.*

Practical sanctification takes place in the present. It is an ongoing process in which God saves you from the power of sin. Through the power of the Holy Spirit within, you can break the chains of sin. As you submit to the Word of God and the promptings of the Spirit, you will become more like God and less like the world. You will learn to say "no" to your flesh and "yes" to God. You will never be sinless in this life, but you can sin less. That is sanctification.

## Glorification

Glorification will take place in the future when you go to Heaven. It is the end of the process of glorious salvation. God will save you from the very presence of sin as you shed this robe of flesh and rise to seize your everlasting prize. All temptation will be left behind along with your mortal body. Think of it! Never again will you fight the lusts of the flesh and the mind. Never again will you succumb to devilish temptation. Never again will you disappoint the Saviour. You will be like Him for you will see Him as He is. At that moment, your salvation will be complete; and you will ever be with the Lord. What a day that will be!

### 3. The SUMMIT of Glorification

What is the result of glorification? Let us examine the Scriptures to learn how all believers will be glorified. Consider this definition of glorification from the *Lexham Glossary of Theology*.

# THE BEAUTY OF GLORIFICATION

Glorification
> The last stage of salvation where believers are conformed fully to the glorified Christ and given a new form that is free from physical and spiritual defect.

Glorification is the last phase of salvation. It is the culmination of all the promises of God. Through death or rapture, every saint will take his place with God in Heaven. Our Lord was "glorified" when He ascended back to Heaven.

**John 7:39**
*(But this spake he of the Spirit, which they that believe on him should receive: for the Holy Ghost was not yet given; because that Jesus was not yet glorified.)*

We will be glorified with Christ. The Old Testament hints at glorification while the New Testament says explicitly that we will be glorified.

**Psalm 73:24**
*Thou shalt guide me with thy counsel, and afterward receive me to glory.*

**Daniel 12:3**
*And they that be wise shall shine as the brightness of the firmament; and they that turn many to righteousness as the stars for ever and ever.*

**Romans 8:17**
*And if children, then heirs; heirs of God, and joint-heirs with Christ; if so be that we suffer with him, that we may be also glorified together.*

**II Thessalonians 1:12**
*That the name of our Lord Jesus Christ may be glorified in you, and ye in him, according to the grace of our God and the Lord Jesus Christ.*

Glorification includes four glorious gifts that we will experience forever.

- **A Glorious State**

Glorification is the perfection of sanctification. It is the final and complete cleansing of the believer. Sin and suffering are left behind. We will live eternally without spot or wrinkle.

**Ephesians 5:27**
*That he might present it to himself a glorious church, not having spot, or wrinkle, or any such thing; but that it should be holy and without blemish.*

As heirs of God and joint heirs with Christ, we will enjoy the riches of God's grace forever.

**Ephesians 2:7**
*That in the ages to come he might shew the exceeding riches of his grace in his kindness toward us through Christ Jesus.*

We will rule and reign with Christ.

**I Corinthians 15:20–28**
*But now is Christ risen from the dead, and become the firstfruits of them that slept. For since by man came death, by man came also the resurrection of the dead. For as in Adam all die, even so in Christ shall all be made alive. But every man in his own order: Christ the firstfruits; afterward they that are Christ's at his coming. Then cometh the end, when he shall have delivered up the kingdom to God, even the Father; when he shall have put down all rule and all authority and power. For he must reign, till he hath put all enemies under his feet. The last enemy that shall be destroyed is death. For he hath put all things under his feet. But when he saith all things are put under him, it is manifest that he is excepted, which did put all things under him. And when all things shall be subdued unto him, then shall the Son also himself be subject unto him that put all things under him, that God may be all in all.*

# THE BEAUTY OF GLORIFICATION

**II Timothy 2:12**
*If we suffer, we shall also reign with him: if we deny him, he also will deny us:*

- **A Glorious Home**

    Christ is preparing us a home in Heaven. It is an amazing place without the corruption of sin.

**John 14:1-3**
*Let not your heart be troubled: ye believe in God, believe also in me. In my Father's house are many mansions: if it were not so, I would have told you. I go to prepare a place for you. And if I go and prepare a place for you, I will come again, and receive you unto myself; that where I am, there ye may be also.*

What does the Bible say about our new home?

**Revelation 21:1-5**
*And I saw a new heaven and a new earth: for the first heaven and the first earth were passed away; and there was no more sea. And I John saw the holy city, new Jerusalem, coming down from God out of heaven, prepared as a bride adorned for her husband. And I heard a great voice out of heaven saying, Behold, the tabernacle of God is with men, and he will dwell with them, and they shall be his people, and God himself shall be with them, and be their God. And God shall wipe away all tears from their eyes; and there shall be no more death, neither sorrow, nor crying, neither shall there be any more pain: for the former things are passed away. And he that sat upon the throne said, Behold, I make all things new. And he said unto me, Write: for these words are true and faithful.*

I cannot wait to get there!

**II Corinthians 5:1**
*For we know that if our earthly house of this tabernacle were dissolved, we have a building of God, an house not made with hands, eternal in the heavens.*

Our heavenly home is a real place.

- **A Glorious Body**

In Heaven, we will have perfect bodies that have not been corrupted by sin and are not bound to the laws of physics as we know them on Earth.

**II Corinthians 5:2–4**
*For in this we groan, earnestly desiring to be clothed upon with our house which is from heaven: If so be that being clothed we shall not be found naked. For we that are in this tabernacle do groan, being burdened: not for that we would be unclothed, but clothed upon, that mortality might be swallowed up of life.*

Christ will give each of us a glorious body made in His likeness. We call this the glorified body.

**Philippians 3:21**
*Who shall change our vile body, that it may be fashioned like unto his glorious body, according to the working whereby he is able even to subdue all things unto himself.*

The most complete passage referring to our heavenly bodies is found in I Corinthians 15.

**I Corinthians 15:35–50**
*But some man will say, How are the dead raised up? and with what body do they come? Thou fool, that which thou sowest is not quickened, except it die: And that which thou sowest, thou sowest not that body that shall be, but bare grain, it may chance of wheat, or of some other grain: But God giveth it a body as it hath pleased him, and to every seed his own body. All flesh is not the same flesh: but there is one kind of flesh of men, another flesh of beasts, another of fishes, and another of birds. There are also celestial bodies, and bodies terrestrial: but the glory of the celestial is one, and the glory of the terrestrial is another. There*

*is one glory of the sun, and another glory of the moon, and another glory of the stars: for one star differeth from another star in glory. So also is the resurrection of the dead. It is sown in corruption; it is raised in incorruption: It is sown in dishonour; it is raised in glory: it is sown in weakness; it is raised in power: It is sown a natural body; it is raised a spiritual body. There is a natural body, and there is a spiritual body. And so it is written, The first man Adam was made a living soul; the last Adam was made a quickening spirit. Howbeit that was not first which is spiritual, but that which is natural; and afterward that which is spiritual. The first man is of the earth, earthy: the second man is the Lord from heaven. As is the earthy, such are they also that are earthy: and as is the heavenly, such are they also that are heavenly. And as we have borne the image of the earthy, we shall also bear the image of the heavenly. Now this I say, brethren, that flesh and blood cannot inherit the kingdom of God; neither doth corruption inherit incorruption.*

Although pertaining to the rapture of the saints, the next verses give us more information about the nature of our glorified bodies.

**I Corinthians 15:51-57**
*Behold, I shew you a mystery; We shall not all sleep, but we shall all be changed, In a moment, in the twinkling of an eye, at the last trump: for the trumpet shall sound, and the dead shall be raised incorruptible, and we shall be changed. For this corruptible must put on incorruption, and this mortal must put on immortality. So when this corruptible shall have put on incorruption, and this mortal shall have put on immortality, then shall be brought to pass the saying that is written, Death is swallowed up in victory. O death, where is thy sting? O grave, where is thy victory? The sting of death is sin; and the strength of sin is the law. But thanks be to God, which giveth us the victory through our Lord Jesus Christ.*

Thank God for a new body! Never again will you feel fatigue, sickness, or pain.

- **A Glorious Eternity**

The zenith of glorification is when God makes all things new.

**Revelation 21:5**
*And he that sat upon the throne said, Behold, I make all things new. And he said unto me, Write: for these words are true and faithful.*

The old ways of sin, defeat, corruption, and suffering will be replaced with a new order of eternal joy and grace. There will be a new Heaven, a new Earth, and a new Jerusalem. God's plan of salvation will be complete.

Wow! God not only saved us from sin and eternal wrath but also promised to share His glory with us. If you are justified, you will be glorified. You will have a glorified state, a glorified home, a glorified body, and a glorious eternity. Our beautiful salvation will climax with our final perfection. We will be transformed into the image of Christ and will live joyfully forever in our new eternal home. Thank God for the beauty of salvation viewed in light of the doctrine of glorification!

# Afterword

## 5 Steps to Heaven

**I John 5:13**
*These things have I written unto you that believe on the name of the Son of God; that ye may know that ye have eternal life, and that ye may believe on the name of the Son of God.*

Nothing in this life matters if you go to Hell when you die. Are you confident that you will go to Heaven? Do you know what the Bible says about securing your place in eternal bliss? God made a way for you to know by faith that you are going to Heaven. You may be closer to Heaven than you think! Only five simple steps separate you from eternal joy in Heaven with God. Follow these steps to settle your eternal destination.

### 1. THINK ABOUT YOUR SOUL.

**Isaiah 1:18**
*Come now, and let us reason together, saith the LORD: though your sins be as scarlet, they shall be as white as snow; though they be red like crimson, they shall be as wool.*

When was the last time you considered the miracle of your existence? Why are you here? Why can you think, reason, and feel far above the animal kingdom? Are you a temporary cosmic accident with no true purpose? Is there nothing beyond the mysterious veil of death? My Friend, you have a lot to think about before you dismiss the afterlife and the eternal destination of your soul!

The Bible teaches that you are a special creation of God. You are here because He wanted you to exist. He has given you an eternal soul that will live forever. Long after your body expires, your soul still will be, will know, and will feel. Your soul includes your personality and the part of you that is reading, understanding these words, and thinking about them right now.

Most people will enter eternity without ever truly thinking about their souls beyond popular quotes, philosophical bullet points, or preconceived ideas. Take the time to learn what God says in the Bible about salvation before you wager your soul on anything else.

**2. Realize the penalty for sin is eternal separation from God in Hell.**

The Law of Consequence is evident in your everyday life. When any law is violated, there is a penalty. Whether you rob a bank or jump off a bridge, consequences will follow. Our Creator not only instituted the laws of nature but also gave humanity a set of moral laws. The most basic of them are found in the Ten Commandments. Just as the laws of nature are in effect even if you do not acknowledge them personally, so are God's laws.

When we break God's law, we are committing sin. Sin separates us from God and condemns us to pay for our sins. Hell is the fiery eternal abode of those who die in their sins in everlasting torment. God does not want you to go to Hell. He made a way for you to go to Heaven when you die.

**Revelation 21:8**
*...and all liars, shall have their part in the lake which burneth with fire and brimstone: which is the second death.*

**Romans 6:23**
*For the wages of sin is death; but the gift of God is eternal life through Jesus Christ our Lord.*

# AFTERWORD

**3. UNDERSTAND THAT JESUS CHRIST DIED ON THE CROSS TO PAY FOR YOUR SINS.**

If you owe money on your electric bill, the electric company does not care who writes the check as long as your account is paid. You owe a debt because of sin. The price is death in Hell. Jesus paid your sin debt on the Cross. When you accept His payment for your sins, your heavenly account is marked "PAID IN FULL" and your home is reserved in Heaven. When He arose on the third day, Christ proved that He was the Son of God and the Saviour of the world Who has power over death.

**I Corinthians 15:3-4**
*For I delivered unto you first of all that which I also received, how that Christ died for our sins according to the scriptures; And that he was buried, and that he rose again the third day according to the scriptures:*

**4. SEE YOUR NEED OF JESUS CHRIST AS YOUR PERSONAL SAVIOUR.**

You are a sinner who has broken God's law. The wrath of God abides on you every moment until you accept Christ's payment for your sins. However, this book in your hand is one more reminder that God is trying to get your attention. God loves you and wants you to spend eternity with Him in Heaven. Nevertheless, if you reject His love, you will face His fierce wrath. You have been warned! Do not refuse His repeated attempts to prove His love for you and to save you. Do you really want to meet God Almighty face-to-face after rejecting His Son's sacrifice for you?

**John 3:36**
*He that believeth on the Son hath everlasting life: and he that believeth not the Son shall not see life; but the wrath of God abideth on him.*

**5. TRUST CHRIST IN YOUR HEART AS YOUR ONLY HOPE FOR HEAVEN.**

# THE BEAUTY OF SALVATION

The Bible is clear that faith in Jesus Christ is God's plan for your salvation. Good intentions and good works can never overcome your sin debt. When you die, God will not let you into Heaven because you were spiritual or religious or because you attended a certain church. You must believe in your heart. Heart belief is more than a mental assent to the facts about the Lord Jesus. It is a personal confidence that Jesus Christ is exactly Who the Bible claims He is that leads you to trust Him with the eternal destiny of your soul.

**The five steps to Heaven are summed up in one word – TRUST.**

**Romans 10:9–13**
*That if thou shalt confess with thy mouth the Lord Jesus, and shalt believe in thine heart that God hath raised him from the dead, thou shalt be saved. For with the heart man believeth unto righteousness; and with the mouth confession is made unto salvation. For the scripture saith, Whosoever believeth on him shall not be ashamed. For there is no difference between the Jew and the Greek: for the same Lord over all is rich unto all that call upon him. For whosoever shall call upon the name of the Lord shall be saved.*

Take the final step right now! If you believe in your heart that Jesus Christ is the Son of God Who died on the Cross for your sin, you should confess your faith in Him right now and ask Him to be your Saviour through prayer. He will see your faith, hear your prayer, and reserve your home in Heaven.

*Dear Jesus, I confess that I am a sinner and that I cannot go to Heaven without You. I do not want to go to Hell. I believe that You are the Son of God Who died on the Cross to pay for my sin, that You were buried, and that You rose again. Please forgive all my sins and take me to Heaven when I die. I am trusting You alone as my way to Heaven. Thank You for saving me. Help me to live for You. Amen.*

Contact me if you chose to trust Christ as Saviour today. I look forward to rejoicing with you!

## About the Author

Paul E. Chapman loves helping committed Christians reach their potential, fulfill God's will, and change their world. He has served as the pastor of Curtis Corner Baptist Church since May of 2004. He and his wife, Sarah, have three precious children and live in a coastal community in the beautiful state of Rhode Island. They have a passion to reach the lost for Christ, to teach believers to live by faith, and to train God's people for the work of the ministry. Sarah has had a unique blend of aggressive autoimmune diseases since 2008 that leaves her bedbound 95% of the time and causes her to be in constant, debilitating pain. Their family's testimony of faithfulness to God has been an encouragement to many. Paul writes weekly on his website and uses his unique blend of talents for God through various ministries and enterprises. Learn more at www.PaulEChapman.com.

**thepaulechapman**

## Also Available from This Author:

## THIS MINI BOOK WILL HELP YOU SEE MORE PEOPLE SAVED.

The mini book *Ye Must Be Born Again* was written to help you fulfill your mission of spreading the Gospel. Whether you are a Christian concerned about your friends and family or a pastor looking for a new tool to help your church win souls, this mini book is for you! It includes a crystal-clear presentation of the Gospel, a moving plea to accept Christ, powerful reasons for assurance of salvation, and first steps for new converts.

Order Yours Today at AddToYourFaith.com

# Also Available from This Author:

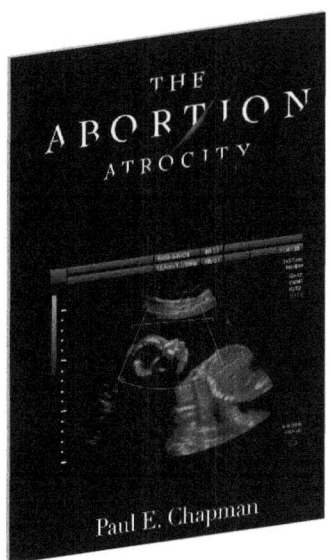

## THIS SHOCKING MINI BOOK SETTLES THE CONTENTIOUS ISSUE OF ABORTION.

*The Abortion Atrocity* exposes the truth behind the evil practice of abortion and gives you ten statements founded on the Word of God that settle the abortion issue. At a time when our nation is at a crossroads, we need to be personally informed and must do what we can to explain God's view on abortion to others.

Get Bulk Discounts at AddToYourFaith.com

## Also Available from This Author:

### JUST SAY NO!
### FORTY DAYS TO
### VICTORY OVER TEMPTATION

This is a devotional book designed to give a daily Minimum Effective Dose (MED) of Bible truth on the subject of temptation. Every chapter is a call to say NO to sin. Trust God for the victory. With His help, you can create lasting, positive change in your life. Once you have the victory, you can help others find it as well.

ORDER YOURS TODAY AT ADDTOYOURFAITH.COM

www.ingramcontent.com/pod-product-compliance
Lightning Source LLC
Chambersburg PA
CBHW071705040426
42446CB00011B/1920